Testimonies of Tragedy and Resistance in the Minsk Ghetto 1941 - 1943

By: Leonid Tsyrinskiy and Anna Machiz

A Publication of JewishGen, INC
Edmond J. Safra Plaza, 36 Battery Place, New York, NY 10280
646.494.5972 | info@JewishGen.org | www.jewishgen.org

JewishGen, Inc. 2023.
An affiliate of New York's Museum of Jewish Heritage – A Living Memorial to the Holocaust

Copyright ©2023 by The Together Plan. All rights reserved.
Published by JewishGen Inc.
First Printing: October 2023, Tishrei 5784

Author: Leonid Tsyrinskiy and Anna Machiz
Translated by: Nick Trapp BA (Hons)
Edited by: Richard Baker, BA (Hons), MBA, FeRSA, CiMgt and Debra Brunner, BA (Hons), AUH, FRSA.
Layout: The Together Plan
Index: Jonathan Wind (JewishGen)
Cover Design: The Together Plan

This book may not be reproduced, in whole or in part, including illustrations in any form (beyond that copying permitted by Sections 107 and 108 of the U.S. Copyright Law and except by reviewers for public press), without written permission from the publisher.

JewishGen INC. is not responsible for inaccuracies or omissions in the original work and makes no representations regarding the accuracy of this work.

Library of Congress Control Number (LCCN): 2023933322

ISBN: 978-1-954176-74-4 (soft cover 164 pages)

About JewishGen.org

JewishGen, an affiliate of the Museum of Jewish Heritage - A Living Memorial to the Holocaust, serves as the global home for Jewish genealogy.

Featuring unparalleled access to 30+ million records, it offers unique search tools, along with opportunities for researchers to connect with others who share similar interests. Award winning resources such as the Family Finder, Discussion Groups, and ViewMate, are relied upon by thousands each day.

In addition, JewishGen's extensive informational, educational, and historical offerings, such as the Jewish Communities Database, Yizkor Book translations, InfoFiles, Family Tree of the Jewish People, and KehilaLinks, provide critical insights, first-hand accounts, and context about Jewish communal and familial life throughout the world.

Offered as a free resource, JewishGen.org has facilitated thousands of family connections and success stories and is currently engaged in an intensive expansion effort that will bring many more records, tools, and resources to its collections.

Please visit https://www.jewishgen.org/ to learn more.

Executive Director: Avraham Groll

About JewishGen Press

JewishGen Press (formerly the Yizkor Books-in-Print Project) is the publishing division of JewishGen.org and provides a venue for the publication of non-fiction books pertaining to Jewish genealogy, history, culture, and heritage.

In addition to the Yizkor Book category, publications in the Other Non-Fiction category include Shoah memoirs and research, genealogical research, collections of genealogical and historical materials, biographies, diaries and letters, studies of Jewish experience and cultural life in the past, academic theses, and other books of interest to the Jewish community.

Please visit https://www.jewishgen.org/Yizkor/ybip.html to learn more.

Director of JewishGen Press: Joel Alpert
Managing Editor - Jessica Feinstein
Publications Manager - Susan Rosin

Geopolitical Information

Minsk is located at 53°54' N 27°34' E.

	Town	District	Province	Country
Before WWI	Minsk	Minsk	Minsk	Russian Empire
Between the Wars	Minsk	Minsk	Belarus SSR	Soviet Union
After WWII	Minsk			Soviet Union
Today (c. 2000):	Minsk			Belarus

Alternate Names for the Town:

Minsk [Bel, Rus, Yid], Mińsk [Pol], Minskas [Lith], Mensk, Miensk

Nearby Jewish Communities:
Samokhvalovichi 12 miles SSW
Astrashytski Haradok 13 miles NNE
Zaslawye 13 miles WNW
Uzlyany 21 miles SSE
Smilavichy 21 miles ESE
Rakov 22 miles WNW
Radashkovichy 22 miles NW
Dukora 22 miles SE
Dzyarzhynsk 23 miles SW
Smalyavichy 23 miles ENE
Lahoysk 24 miles NNE
Hajna 24 miles NNE
Rudensk 24 miles SSE
Krasnae 30 miles NW

Jewish Population in 1900: 48,000

Map of Belarus showing the location of **Minsk**

The Johannes Rau Minsk International Education Centre
The Dortmund International Education Centre
The Johannes Rau MMOTs Historical Studio

Anna Machiz

Testimonies of Tragedy and Resistance in the Minsk Ghetto 1941-1943

Minsk
Publisher: I. P. Logvinov
2011

UDC 94(=411.16)(476-25)"1941/1943(093.3)
BBK 63.3(4Bei)622
A68

Compiled by L. A. Tsyrinskiy
Edited by K. I. Kozak, Candidate of Sciences (History), Senior Lecturer

Editorial board:
V. F. Balakirev, Candidate of Sciences (Philology), Director of The Johannes Rau Minsk International Education Centre
Peter Junge-Wentrup, Manager of The Dortmund International Education Centre (Germany)
L. M. Levin, Chairman of the Union of Belarusian Jewish Public Associations and Communities
Professor Manfred Zabel, Chairman of the General Meeting of members of The Johannes Rau Minsk International Education Centre

Reviewer
Professor V. K. Korshuk, Doctor of Sciences (History)

A68   Anna Machiz: Testimonies of Tragedy and Resistance in the Minsk Ghetto, 1941-1943 / compiled by L. A. Tsyrinskiy; ed. K. I. Kozak. – Minsk: I. P. Logvinov, 2011. – 106 s.

ISBN 978-985-6991-53-3.

Documentary testimonies by former inmate of the Minsk Ghetto, member of the underground and partisan Anna Machiz, containing little-known passages about the history of tragedies and struggles in the Minsk Ghetto from 1941 to 1943, reproduced following the Nazis' liquidation of the Minsk Ghetto, the largest in Europe, at the end of 1943. Documentary materials, articles and illustrations have been provided as a supplement.
This book is intended for historians, specialists and anyone treating the subject of Holocaust history.

UDC 94(=411.16)(476-25)"1941/1943(093.3)
BBK 63.3(4Bei)622

ISBN 978-985-6991-53-3.   © L. A. Tsyrinskiy, compilation, 2011
© Historical workshop by The Johannes Rau Minsk International Education Centre, 2011
© Design. Publisher: I. P. Logvinov, 2011

The Together Plan Charity

The Together Plan is a charity registered with the UK Charity Commission for England and Wales. The charity's mission is community capacity building in the former Soviet Union countries through the lens of Jewish cultural heritage and education, with a current focus (at the time of writing in 2023) on Jewish Belarus.

It is our vision that Belarus's seven hundred years of Jewish history will ultimately be acknowledged globally, and Belarusian Jews and non-Jews will feel empowered to participate in citizen-led programmes that will bring this history into focus. In this way, self-sustaining projects will ultimately help Belarusian Jewish communities to gain recognition and thrive.

Our charity's programmes help to develop the capacity and skills of members of Jewish communities in Belarus, in such a way that they are better able to identify, and help meet their own needs, and to participate more fully in society. Non-Jewish people are also participating in the charity's programmes.

A key strategic aim of the charity is to engage Belarusian citizens in the participation of programmes that help them to discover and tell the history of the Jews of Belarus, so that they can pass it on to others. This will encourage discourse and build connections to Belarusian Jews and people in the diaspora, so that they too can play an active role in this global project. The goal is to help create an awareness, understanding and appreciation of the importance of the history of Jewish Belarus to the wider world.

Our programmes promote dialogue and empowerment, encourage community development, and help Jewish people come back and reconnect to their lost culture, their traditions, and their heritage.

The Together Plan is working to build a Belarusian Jewish Heritage Route as part of the *European Route of Jewish Heritage*, which is managed by the AEPJ (European Association for the Preservation and Promotion of Jewish Heritage and Culture). The *European Route of Jewish Heritage* is one of the certified routes of the Council of Europe's Cultural Routes Programme.

The Together Plan has created a Holocaust education programme in Belarus and the UK called **Making History Together**, which shines a light on the hidden history of the Holocaust in Belarus and the Soviet Union.

The charity, in partnership with its sister non-profit in the USA, **Jewish Tapestry Project**, aims to mark, and where possible, restore Jewish heritage sites in Belarus.

Translating books that shed new light on the little-known history of the Holocaust in Belarus is a vital part of The Together Plan's work, and we feel privileged that Leonid Tsyrinskiy entrusted his book to us. It has been an honour to be able to bring it to the English-speaking world.

The Together Plan (UK)
UK Charity 1154167

Jewish Tapestry Project (USA)
USA non-profit 501(C)3 organization

www.thetogetherplan.com

www.jewishtapestryproject.org

Acknowledgements

Neil Adams, Senior Lecturer Spatial Planning, London South Bank University, for contextualising some material for audiences unfamiliar with Belarus.

Richard Baker BA (Hons), MBA, FeRSA, CiMgt, for his diligent commitment to the editing of the English draft.

Jack Baum, Trustee of The Together Plan for his invaluable assistance with formatting the text and technical support.

Hilda Bronstein PhD, for the creation of the glossary.

Debra Brunner BA (Hons), AUH, FRSA, for bringing the book back with her from Minsk, for the initiative, oversight, and determination in bringing this book to life.

Artur Livshyts, for coordinating the research in Belarus, for his undying commitment to the Minsk Ghetto survivors and his unfailing determination to tell the story of the Minsk Ghetto.

Vladimir Melnitskiy, for writing the Foreword and for his consultancy on the project.

Bernie Nyman, B.M.Nyman & Co, Publishing Lawyers, for his guidance.

Susan Rosin and the team at the Jewish Gen Yizkor Book Project, for their guidance and partnership in the publication of the book.

Sonya Shaipak, a valued member of The Together Plan team in Minsk, for her tireless assistance with managing the editing queries, doing additional translations, and formatting the photographs.

Lydia Speakman, BA (Hons), MPhil, for proofreading the text.

Faizal Sulthan (Unsplash), for backdrop image for the book cover.

Nick Trapp BA (Hons), for translating the original Russian text.

Leonid Tsyrinskiy (Minsk), for bringing this book to our attention and for his invaluable assistance with the editing queries.

Sonya Zuckerman LL.B (Hons), for doing the final read through of the text.

Staff and volunteers at The Together Plan, for their general assistance and support throughout.

The Streets of My Childhood

"I grew up in the area where the Minsk Ghetto was located. It is hard to imagine that such brutal and inhuman crimes were once committed on the streets of my childhood. There are elderly people still alive today, still living in Minsk who were children imprisoned in the Minsk Ghetto. They witnessed it all, all the horrors and they endured unthinkable losses. Their childhood, unlike mine, was a very different experience. The ghetto was located in the city centre, and today these survivors have to walk the streets of their painful past. It is impossible for them to go back to their childhood homes because most of the buildings were destroyed, but what would they be going back to? Empty spaces where everyone and everything you loved was destroyed.

The history of the Minsk Ghetto through the eyes of its prisoner Anna Machiz should be accepted with gratitude and respect."

Artur Livshyts,
Co-founder and Country Director of The Together Plan Charity,
Chair of the Jewish Religious Union of Belarus,
Minsk, Belarus, 2022

Table of Contents

	Page
Preface, Debra Brunner, BA (Hons), FRSA	2
Foreword, Vladimir Melnitskiy	6
Translator's introduction, Nick Trapp, BA (Hons)	9
Editor's introduction, Richard Baker, BA (Hons), MBA, FeRSA, CiMgt	11
Context for an English-speaking audience, Neil Adams, Senior lecturer Spatial Planning, London South Bank University	13
Section 1. The Minsk Ghetto: history, memory, culture	26
Repaying a debt, Leonid Tsyrinskiy	27
The tragedy of the Minsk Ghetto: the first testimonies of Anna Machiz, Kuzma Kozak	29
A Woman of Legend: Criminal Investigator for the NKVD of the BSSR and Chronicler of the Underground in the Minsk Ghetto, Professor E.G Ioffe	35
Section 2. The Minsk Ghetto as remembered by Anna Machiz	48
Appendix to the memoirs of Anna Semyonovna Machiz (Levina)	89
Section 3. Supporting publications and documents	98
Publications	99
Documents	106
Section 4. Photos	117
Glossary of terms	136
Gallery of archive images	143
Index of names	148

Preface

*"How do we even begin to try to understand the Holocaust in its entirety? The full story from beginning to end. In truth, 'the Holocaust' for most people conjures images of the death and concentration camps of Poland and Auschwitz-Birkenau, the focus of Hitler's 'Final Solution'. Film footage, photographs, survivor testimonies and eyewitness accounts from the liberating forces in Poland, ensured that these places would never be forgotten. But what of the atrocities where no liberating ever reached and where hardly anyone survived? What about the citizens of the Soviet Union who did return from camps, hiding places, forests, but never told of their suffering or losses because to do so risked persecution or incarceration? What of the lands between Poland and Moscow, that battleground and its people; the places no-one talks of, because no-one knows what happened there. Auschwitz was the **final** solution which in itself tells us there had been other solutions. What were they and why don't we learn about them?"*

Timothy Snyder,
Bloodlands,
2010

In 2014 I met, for the first time, a group of survivors from the Minsk Ghetto. The meeting took place in Minsk with this extraordinary group of people who had never left the place where they had experienced so much loss and had witnessed so many atrocities. These elderly people were children when Germany invaded the Soviet Union on 22nd June 1941. Their book, a collection of privately published memories of life in the Minsk Ghetto (in Russian), was gifted to me at that first meeting. The minute that book was placed in my hands I knew there was work to be done. It took four years to bring 'We Remember Lest the World Forget - Memories of the Minsk Ghetto' to the English-speaking world, an ambitious and demanding translation project. It was an unbelievable journey, fraught with personal challenges that almost derailed the project and there were moments when I was unsure we were ever going to make it. Yet somehow, we persevered and found ways to overcome the obstacles. As the stories slowly took shape, the mist lifted from the Russian as the English words settled onto the pages, the enormity of the significance of this little-known history loomed large. These were just short modest excerpts of people's memories - people who as children had witnessed horrors in the darkest moments of the 20th century, people who had been silenced after the war. Jewish survivors in the Soviet Union were treated as all Soviet citizens. The suffering was collective - all Soviet's together. There was no separate story of Jewish suffering. The impact that this book's translation had on the survivors was immense. It gave them a real sense of empowerment and strength to know that their stories were now available to be read across the world.

As we were bringing 'We Remember Lest the World Forget' to publication, I was back in Minsk. It was early 2018, and one of the survivors, Leonid Tsyrinskiy, handed me a book. He was polite and softly spoken and he quietly asked if I would translate this one too. He had a look of deep yearning in his eyes, and I could see that this meant a lot to him and that it was really important. I took the book, acknowledging my gratitude and at that time - was so overwhelmed with the extent of work that the current book had presented me with, that I was unsure when I would ever be able to find the time to do a second. I took this little book back to the UK with me and placed it on my desk where it sat for two years.

Through years of running summer programmes and visiting communities in Belarus, it was painfully clear that few in the country had an awareness of their own Jewish history and Holocaust history. Certainly outside of Belarus, there was little about this history within mainstream education or Holocaust education. Was this history at risk of never seeing the light of day?

In 2013 I co-founded The Together Plan Charity along with Artur Livshyts, who lives in Minsk. The mission of the charity is community capacity building in former Soviet Union countries through the lens of Jewish cultural heritage and education, with a current focus on Jewish Belarus. Years of working in Belarus has taught us that people in the country, Jews and non-Jews, have a burning desire to explore and understand the Jewish history of their country. For us to help them, it became an imperative for us to explore and understand that heritage ourselves: and for us to succeed in our mission as a charity, we needed to share those stories.

At the end of 2019, I devised an education programme for young learners in Belarus and beyond and called it 'Making History Together'. We found support for the programme which explores the history of the Jews of Belarus and the Holocaust between 1941 and 1944, and I brought in a co-creator, Leo Levine. Then the world was hit by COVID. As we all withdrew to the safety of our own homes and grew socially isolated, the book on my desk suddenly drew my attention. I immediately contacted one of our trusted volunteers, Nick Trapp, who had recently completed his degree in European and Middle Eastern Languages at Oxford University. Nick, a fluent Russian speaker who had been to Belarus with me on a number of occasions, was happy to take my call. When asked how COVID has impacted him, he readily told me he was on furlough and unable to work. When I asked him if he might have time to translate a book about the Minsk Ghetto - he was all too happy to accept the task and the book was posted to Bristol. As Leo and I worked diligently and virtually on the 'Making History Together' programme, Nick was translating in the safety of his home. Socially distanced, we were a team hard at work - truly an industrious hive of activity.

It has taken three years to bring 'Anna Machiz, Testimonies of Tragedy and Resistance in the Minsk Ghetto 1941-1943' to completion. There have been months dedicated to making multiple edits, sending queries to historians and survivors, to Leonid Tsyrinskiy, the team in Minsk, to Nick Trapp and so much more.

What happens now with this little book that Leonid Tsyrinskiy entrusted to my care in early 2018? I now understand the look of deep yearning in Leonid's eyes. This book is beyond important. In every way I feel honoured and privileged that we have been able to bring this book into the light and I hope that Anna Machiz's name will be elevated in the ranks among the better-known names of partisans and Minsk Ghetto resistance fighters. Anna's name fell into anonymity and undeservedly so. Leonid Tsyrinskiy has brought Anna's memoir back from the depths. It was locked away in the KGB archives at risk of being forgotten. Anna's writings - captured on a typewriter in the Naliboki Forest during her time with the partisans give us a raw and detailed insight into the sheer brutality of the Minsk Ghetto. The things she witnessed and what she endured were all meticulously detailed. With thanks to Anna Machiz, we learn how against all the odds, and faced with daily murders on an unfathomable scale, Jews gathered strength to form a ghetto resistance movement. We learn how Jews within the ghetto and non-Jewish communists outside of the ghetto worked together in an attempt to foil their common enemy. Through unbelievable resilience and mental strength in the face of utter horror; devastation and death; and against all odds - Jewish prisoners of the ghetto resisted. Some miraculously escaped, joined partisan detachments in the dense Belarusian forests and continued to fight and play a major role in disrupting the German war machine.

Only 200 copies of this book were ever printed in Russian. Bringing it to the English-speaking world will help more people garner a deeper understanding of the Holocaust in the Soviet Union. To understand the Holocaust - you have to know what happened in the East.

> "Present-day Belarus, from Brest in the west to Vitebsk in the northeast, once constituted a centerpiece of Jewish culture in Europe, inclusive of top-drawer rabbinical academies, of first-rank literature and journalism of linguistic hothouses in which the development of both Hebrew and Yiddish could flower, and so much more. An understanding of modern Jewish life is inseparable from Belarus. The Together Plan is so vital in making this recognition and rediscovery an essential part of twenty-first century discourse."
>
> **Michael Skakun,**
> author, translator, memoirist, and public affairs consultant,
> New York, USA, 2022

There is so much more we need to explore and learn about the Minsk Ghetto, the Holocaust in the Soviet Union, and the history of the Jews of Belarus. At The Together Plan, we believe we need to do this in collaboration with the people of Belarus because this is their history - their story. This is our task.

Debra Brunner,
Founder and CEO,
The Together Plan Charity,
London, UK

Foreword

I am often asked why the Minsk Ghetto was a more horrific concentration camp than Auschwitz, Buchenwald, or Dachau? In Buchenwald a prisoner got a portion of food and a place on the bunk beds, but the Minsk Ghetto was a place of death and nothing else. We were only murdered there.

"The first winter was extremely cold, and the stoves were not heated: where could the firewood be found? The furniture was already burnt. The water supply was destroyed. The prisoners were dying from bullets and bayonets, as well as from hunger, cold, disease... The ghetto was surrounded by rusty barbed wire. The Nazis and the police shot at the citizens who tried to give us food... Memory is also the weapon with which we fight for kindness."

Frida Reizman,
former child prisoner of the Minsk Ghetto,
aged 5 and 8 months in June 1941,
Minsk, Belarus

The Jewish people have a long rich history. Jews are called the 'People of the Book', but they can also be called the 'People of Remembrance'. Jewish remembrance is in many ways universal.

Humans are built in such a way that they remember moments of joy and happiness, dignity, and nobility most often, and do not want to remember things that are associated with negative memories - meanness, cruelty, heartlessness. When they are reminded of it, they feel either guilt or despair. Memories of the Holocaust belong to the latter memory. It seems to me that readers of Anna Machiz's book "Testimonies of Tragedy and Resistance in the Minsk Ghetto 1941-1943" will feel the same way, and there will be no indifferent ones.

According to experts, as of June 1, 1941, 9,183,400 people lived in the Byelorussian Soviet Socialist Republic (BSSR), of whom 1,220,000 were Jews. As is well known, Belarusian Jews were a solid majority of the urban population of the Republic, but during the two years of Nazi occupation the history of Belarusian Jewry was savagely interrupted and tragically ended in the fires of the Holocaust.

According to the underestimates of contemporary Belarusian researchers, during the Great Patriotic War no less than 915,000 Jews, or 75% of the pre-war Jewish population of the Republic, were violently killed on the territory of the BSSR. As one of the largest places of extermination of Jews, Minsk is second only to death camps Auschwitz-Birkenau in Auschwitz (1.1 million Jews) and Treblinka (over 850,000) and surpasses Majdanek (over 360,000) and Sobibor (about 250,000) in the number of victims. In the death camp Maly Trostenets, Blagovshchina tract, around 196,000 Belarusian and European Jews and their families, as well as Soviet prisoners of war of Jewish origin, were shot and burnt in a crematorium in Shashkovka near Minsk. From September 1941, Minsk, as the centre of the General District "Beloruthenia", became not only one of the epicentres of the mass genocide of Belarusian (Soviet) Jews, but also the first and largest centre of the secret deportation and murder of German and Nazi-occupied European Jews. From November 1941 to September 1943 about 77,000 European Jews (including non-Jewish husbands and wives) were murdered in Minsk, and up to 93,000 in the entire Republic.

Nearly 173,000 martyrs, including European Jews, passed through the Minsk Ghetto. This largest Jewish death camp in the occupied Union of Soviet Socialist Republics (USSR) was called "hell on Earth". In terms of the number of prisoners it surpassed the Lwów Ghetto (the second largest ghetto in the USSR - 143,000 prisoners) and was second only to the Warsaw Ghetto (around 500,000) and the Łódź Ghetto (over 204,000). In total, more than a million Jews were killed in the Holocaust in Belarus.

Now there is nothing to remind us about the predominance of the Jewish population in almost all Belarusian cities, towns, and settlements. Only memorials, obelisks, monuments, and memorial signs in places of mass extermination of people. Women and men, children and the elderly testify to this fact. Nowadays the number of Belarusian citizens of Jewish origin does not exceed 11,500. There are no more than 6,000 Jews living in Minsk[1].

This little book by Anna Machiz is not just about the tragedy of the Minsk Ghetto. This book is about the sorrow of a long-suffering minority group; about the biggest and most terrible tragedy in human history; about the criminal genocide and mass collaboration; about the victims and survivors of those times when culture, faith and civilisation ceased to exist and only "naked human nature" remained.

Unfortunately, there are many people today who believe that the Holocaust is a previous page of our history, an echo of the past that has faded into oblivion... Yes, that is also true: there are fewer and fewer people interested in this topic. Yet for my generation, the first post-war generation whose parents miraculously survived the Shoah, the Holocaust has gone nowhere, it has become

---

[1] Based on an official enquiry to the National Statistical Committee of the Republic of Belarus submitted in 2021.

a symbol of the most heinous crime of people against people in history. The search for the historical truth and research on this topic must continue, because fascism must not be revived in Europe, where most of the victims of the war were Jews killed by local people...

There were righteous people, but there were also many scoundrels and murderers. This terrible and regrettable fact should not be forgotten in the human "collective memory", because the Holocaust is neither a myth nor a legend. It is a shared tragedy, filled with loss and pain.

Why is it so important for us to remember this? It is important to know the sorrowful and painful truth of the past in order to discover the unknown and see the present, to understand ourselves and learn how to create a better future. It is important to feel the interconnectedness of everything and everyone because such human tragedies should unite people into one whole, called Humanity. We, who are alive, owe the innocent victims a debt of remembrance and sorrow.

We have a duty to know of and remember; the unmarked mass graves of Maly Trostenets, Yama and the Jewish cemetery on Sukhaya Street in Minsk, Babi Yar in Kiev, the names of the victims on the walls of the old synagogue in Prague, the metal plates all over Germany with engraved names of the martyred and disappeared, the inscriptions on memorial signs in Vienna mentioning the thousands of deported to places from which no one returned... Anna Machiz's book is therefore for all of us, for all people of goodwill, regardless of their place of living, nationality, social status, political views, or religion.

For thousands of years, Jews in various territories have been subjected to oppression, discrimination, and bloody pogroms. They have been expelled from their countries, hanged, stabbed, gassed, strangled, burned alive, and their torn bodies burned in crematoriums... They were killed just because they were Jews...

Yet one would like to believe and hope that antisemitism will sooner or later become a thing of the past, just as hatred of other nations will become an atavism, a dirty, shameful, and immoral thing. What kind of future will we have? No one knows what the future holds for all of us, but I am convinced that there must not and will not be any reason for fear.

Vladimir Melnitskiy,
historian, writer, Holocaust researcher and author,
Minsk, Belarus

Translator's introduction

As I write from the relative safety of the UK in 2022, the news is full of coverage of our largest rail strike in 30 years. At some point, one of the reporters must have used the term "summer of discontent". You can now hear it repeated on the television and radio and read it online or in a newspaper. This isn't just journalistic laziness: we all do it. Describing a new event for the first time is difficult, so if someone else comes up with words or phrases that convey its essence better than we could do ourselves, we copy them. Sometimes, we don't even remember who it was who used them in the first place. To use a more light-hearted example, millennials in the UK will unanimously agree on the difference between "going out" and "going out out": the first is a pint of beer or maybe a meal, the second means a trip to a nightclub and a punishing hangover. When we use these terms, we aren't always thinking of the Micky Flanagan comedy sketch that made them famous. Micky was maybe not the first person to coin them, but it was thanks to his platform that they became part of our cultural dialogue about what it means to be British.

The writings of Anna Machiz about the Minsk Ghetto can hardly be compared to either of these examples. Sadly, the cultural dialogue about what it means to be a Belarusian Jew is punctuated by events which are horrific and traumatising. Some passages were difficult to translate not due to their complexity, but because the images they held were so graphic that the words were uncomfortable to write. I hope I have been true to what Anna Machiz would want us to know about the atrocities committed in Belarus under Nazi occupation. But what Anna Machiz does have in common with my examples above is that she was a pioneer who had a hand in creating the vocabulary through which this part of Belarus's history would be talked about in years to come. Kuzma Kozak notes in his literature review that her account was "repeated by great public commentators, historians, and even eyewitnesses of the events in their own narratives about the tragedy, although they did not always cite their source". This is not plagiarism; opening a dialogue about a genocide which happened to your people is a mammoth task. I see Anna Machiz as an enabling figure who gave other survivors of the tragedy words to express the inexpressible. As such it is hard to overstate her importance as a voice in Belarus's history.

Anna Machiz was not a "writer" as such, but a dedicated public prosecutor. This fact both gives the text a frank straightforwardness and endows it with a bitter purpose: to document and bear witness to each and every crime committed against the inhabitants of the Minsk Ghetto, as well as the constant struggle of life within the ghetto itself. As if the Nazis did not make life hard enough, not all of her fellow inmates could be trusted either. Anna Machiz was a realist who made sense of the actions of both the German occupiers and her neighbours in the ghetto through the lens of a criminal psychologist. In her words, "shared misfortunes bring people together, but they can also drive a wedge between them: one must look this unpleasant truth in the face. There are people who start to think only about saving their own skin, and the lower instincts come to the surface…" In such dire circumstances it takes a true hero to think not only about saving their own skin, but also to take the fantastical risk of fighting back and helping others to escape.

I would like to dedicate this translation to the Cherepanov family, my friends from Polotsk and all of the deeply generous people who made it possible for me to spend some time living in Belarus in 2013. Without your merciless corrections my Russian would never have become good enough to translate a book like this.

Nick Trapp,
Editor,
Bristol, UK, 2020 (first COVID-19 lockdown)

Editor's introduction

Being invited to help edit Anna Machiz's memoir of the tragedy and ultimate liquidation of the Minsk Ghetto was a great privilege, and a task to be taken on with great respect.

It is a very important work which contributes to the wider recording of the horror and brutality of the Holocaust. It sits alongside the many, many tragic stories of the events which defiled our continent during the late 1930's and early 1940's, set in the context of 6 years of brutal war.

These stories are all too familiar and shocking, scarring countries and communities across the continent, and they have been recorded through the written word, in official documents, and in pictures, film and video testimony. They are now also increasingly marked by collective and individual monuments as efforts are intensified to ensure that the Holocaust is marked and cannot be forgotten, as the number of people living with personal memory fades.

Whilst at one level this book can be seen as but one contribution to this wider record, it adds substantively in three distinctive ways:

Firstly, it tells the story of one of the largest, but least well documented, episodes of the Holocaust, bearing witness to the death of 100,000 people from across Belarus and beyond who were held, humiliated, and murdered in Minsk by Nazi Germany and its collaborators. From Anna's experience of being present during the events swirling around her, it clearly captures the shock and confusion of the early days of the ghetto, the development of the processes of control and repression of the population, and of the disbelief of its victims.

Secondly, there is a personal quality which is novel about Anna Machiz's account. It was this factor which made me immediately accept the invitation to help bring this text to a wider audience. As a volunteer with the Together Plan, which works to enhance understanding of Jewish history and culture in Belarus and its communities, and as a descendent of a Jewish family who fled this territory in a previous generation, a stand-out aspect of Anna's text is the way it captures the stories and character of real, everyday people – men, women and children – caught up in dangerous events beyond their control. It gives them names, addresses, and occupations. It reaches into their roles and relationships before the War as doctors, teachers, workers and even as criminals. It brings to life their daily existence in the new and terrible context of the ghetto. It details the many ways that these lives were ended, of how people were taken from their homes and forced into the ghetto, how families and friendships were shattered, and the progressive reality of confusion, fear, disconnection and ultimately death.

Whilst many of the murders were random, as the occupying forces exerted their power, often quite casually, it also highlights how identities were used in the design of the progression of the campaign of extermination, sorting people by their occupations, genders, location and capabilities as they selected people to live and die.

Thirdly, it relates the grim determination of those who came together in response, and who organised resistance, both from within this ghetto and through anti-fascist allies amongst the Minsk population. Through Anna's position within this resistance, we can witness a detailed account of a movement developing and acting in real time.

We see the growing determination to fight back, and the steps taken to bring hope. The book describes how these everyday people come together to produce and distribute propaganda, to secure the escape of individuals, to organise action, and to source food and equipment for the partisans. It also describes the nature of the organisation, its priorities and the strategies developed to manage the risk of discovery, betrayal, and penetration of their network. It gives identity to people who accepted the inherent danger of their choice to resist and were willing to trust and protect their comrades in the organisational form they took.

Now that this memoir has been made available after many years of being hidden away, it is these aspects of the account that we have sought to give prominence to in the editorial approach we have taken. Important early sections of the book introduce Anna Machiz and her family, background, and career, tell how this memoir was protected by her relatives, and explain the role and importance of her testimony alongside a small group of other accounts of the Minsk Ghetto and the events in Belarus.

Most importantly the aim has been to give focus and prominence to the authentic voice of Anna Machiz and her account of these events. It is hoped that by presenting her contemporaneous memoir as it was written, her recounting of those she knew and worked with and of the terrible things she witnessed, it in turn validates her experiences and of those who lived and died in the Minsk Ghetto. I hope we have been successful in that task.

Richard Baker,
BA (Hons), MBA, FeRSA, CiMgt,
Newcastle upon Tyne, UK

Context for an English-speaking audience

The aim of this contribution to the book is to try to provide some brief insights into the broader context in relation to Belarus and Minsk with particular reference to the Holocaust in the East[2] and the Minsk Ghetto. The contribution will hopefully be useful to an English-speaking audience who may be unfamiliar with the country and its complex and often traumatic history up to and including the Holocaust. There are fundamental differences between the more familiar Western Front and the War of Annihilation that the Nazis unleashed in the Soviet Union, which resulted in the horrors of the Minsk Ghetto. The scale of the losses and destruction in Belarus and the rest of the Soviet Union are difficult for us in the West to comprehend, estimates vary from 20-30 million civilian and military losses. Contrary to the official Soviet narrative, the suffering of the wider Soviet population and the specific suffering of the Soviet Jews differ fundamentally, one of many reasons why this book is so important.

A brief overview of the relevant history of Belarus is provided with a particular focus on the evolution and role of the significant Jewish communities in numerous centres including Minsk and the impact of the Sovietisation of Belarus. I have sought to differentiate between the Holocaust that most in the West are familiar with, focusing primarily on Auschwitz, and the Holocaust in the East. Some of the key characteristics of Minsk and the Minsk Ghetto that provided the conditions that the prisoners of the Ghetto and members of the Jewish Resistance experienced will be discussed before the structure of the book is explained. I have drawn on my own experiences and on some of the relatively few English language sources about the Holocaust in the East and the few accounts that focus specifically on the Minsk Ghetto.

A glimpse at the history of Belarus

Tracing the evolution of modern-day Belarus is complex and challenging. The territory of modern-day Belarus was incorporated into the Grand Duchy of Lithuania in the thirteenth Century, which at its height in the fifteenth Century was the largest state in Europe covering much of modern-day Belarus, Ukraine, Lithuania and parts of Latvia and Poland. The power of the Grand Duchy and later the Polish-Lithuanian Commonwealth protected its constituent parts from the rule of the Mongols who had invaded much of Kievan Rus in the thirteenth Century. Although there remained significant cultural and linguistic ties with Russia, Belarus was not incorporated into the Russian Empire until the start of

---

[2] I use this term as a general term referring to the Holocaust in the occupied territories of the Soviet Union, including Belarus and the Holocaust in Eastern Europe more generally.

the nineteenth Century. During this period a conscious Byelorussian identity started to consolidate, despite fluctuating periods of Russification.

Belarus was also central to the Pale of Settlement, a Western region of the Russian Empire where Jews were allowed to live permanently resulting in a much higher proportion of Jews in the population than in other areas of the Russian Empire where Jews were generally not allowed to register as permanent residents. The Pale of Settlement was disbanded at the end of World War 1 with the collapse of the Russian Empire, but at its height was home to over 5 million Jews (Arad 2009), estimated to be about 40% of the world Jewish population at the time. The establishment of the Pale created the conditions for the Holocaust in the East as it concentrated the majority of Europe's Jews in this area (Arad 2009, Wade-Beorn 2018).

The origins of the book, elements of the local context and the key characters in the book are introduced by various key players in the introductory pages. Belarus as a country and therefore its history and particularly the fate of the Jews in the Holocaust remain somewhat hidden and therefore mysterious for many Western readers. We in the West can tend to consider Eastern Europe as a unified, coherent, and somewhat homogenous region, which could not be further from the truth. Whilst Eastern Europe has experienced numerous conflicts and changes of borders and political systems, these have had diverse impacts in different places. The location of Belarus sandwiched between Russia to the east, Ukraine to the south, Poland to the west and Latvia and Lithuania to the north-west underlie the reasons for its complex and often traumatic history.

The chaos during and in the aftermath of World War 1 saw extensive conflicts between the competing powers of Germany, the Soviet Union and Poland before the Byelorussian[3] Soviet Socialist Republic emerged from the wreckage. Being a fully-fledged Soviet Socialist Republic from the 1920s onwards meant that there was a limited consciousness and awareness of Belarus in the West. Population movements and the fluidity of the national borders are another reason why this part of the world remains something of a mystery to many.

---

[3] The terms Belorussia and Belarus translate roughly as White Russia in the Russian language. Belorussia was used in the time off the Russian Empire. After integration into the Soviet Union, it became known as the Byelorussian Soviet Socialist Republic, so the official historical name is used here. Since independence in 1990 the country is most commonly referred to as the Republic of Belarus, although Belorussia is still commonly used in some countries.

The Sovietisation of Belarus

The incorporation of Belarus into the Soviet Union in the 1920s differed significantly to the occupation of the Baltic states in the aftermath of World War 2. The earlier incorporation of Belarus was relatively peaceful and voluntary in comparison to the occupation of the Baltic states primarily due to closer cultural and linguistic ties. By the outbreak of World War 2 Belarus and the population had experienced over two decades of Soviet rule and Epstein (2008) among others characterised pre-war Belarus as having relatively harmonious relations between Jewish and non-Jewish communities in comparison to neighbouring countries where overt and covert antisemitism were more widespread. The closer cultural and linguistic relations between Belarus and Russia were consolidated during these two decades when Belarussian citizens were exposed to the internationalist spirit of the early Soviet Union that promoted the idea of internationalisation and encouraged the assimilation of Jews and non-Jews.

There are a number of other important consequences of this period of Sovietisation that would impact life in the Minsk Ghetto and differentiate it from other large Ghettos further west. Walke (2015) explores the specific experiences of young people during the Holocaust in Belarus and dedicates an insightful chapter to the experiences of young Soviet Jews in the Minsk Ghetto, summed up perfectly by a quote from survivor Vera Smirnova:

"….. my childhood didn't last very long. Childhood was when people were burned and killed" (Walke 2015: 68) and Walke herself referred to the Minsk Ghetto as being "a life immersed in death" (Walke ibid: 69).

She argues that this first generation growing up in early Soviet Belarus in an environment that promoted assimilation had not experienced extreme forms of antisemitism and the consequences of pogroms, war, and revolution and that therefore the Holocaust undermined much of their pre-war identity and understanding of the world. Ironically the forcing together of Jews into the Minsk Ghetto in some ways led to the revival of Jewish cultural and religious traditions and institutions, which Soviet policy had sought to dismantle. Although there are accounts of antisemitism in Belarus at this time, the relatively harmonious pre-war relations between Jews and non-Jews provided foundations for the extensive co-operation between the Jewish Ghetto Resistance and a much larger non-Jewish communist Resistance in the city and wider region.

The War of Annihilation and the Holocaust in the East

The scale and barbaric nature of the losses of civilians and military in Belarus and the wider occupied Soviet territories are difficult for us in the West to comprehend. The invading Nazis disregarded any semblance of restraint that they had shown in Western Europe towards the local population in their War of Annihilation in the Soviet Union. The cynical Generalplan Ost outlined the Nazi aims of systematically murdering approximately 30 million people deliberately using hunger, violence, and death as strategies to break the spirit and physical resilience of the Jews. The Nazi leadership justified their brutality towards the civilian population by claiming that they were legitimate targets as they supported the Partisans. Though estimates vary it is thought that approximately 9200 villages and hundreds of towns in Belarus were burned to the ground along with most or all of the local population. Approximately one quarter of the 9 million pre-war population of Belarus are thought to have died during the War.

    In the post-war period many memoirs and accounts from Minsk and other Ghetto's and killing sites were locked in Soviet archives which were generally inaccessible to Western researchers. In addition, the nature of the official Soviet narrative in the post-war years deprived Jews of their specific identity in relation to the suffering, absorbing their very specific suffering into the overall suffering of the Soviet people. Although the non-Jewish population of Belarus suffered terribly under the Nazis, the denial and lack of official recognition of the specific and fundamentally different nature and extent of the Jewish suffering meant that many Ghetto survivors suffered in silence after the War. Walke (2015) argues that this lack of official recognition in the post-war period was exacerbated for certain groups, namely women and children, whose pivotal roles in the Ghetto Resistance and the Partisans were rarely acknowledged officially. The accounts of Anna Machiz in this book and the memoirs of other survivors in 'We Remember Lest the World Forget – Memories of the Minsk Ghetto' therefore take on added importance.

    Belarus became an independent Republic in 1990 in the wake of the collapse of the Soviet Union but even in subsequent years the country has remained relatively closed to Western eyes in terms of tourism, trade, and cultural ties. Although there has been an increased consciousness and awareness of the specific suffering of Soviet Jews since 1990, much of the impetus for this has come from the Jewish diaspora and a relatively small band of committed survivors and researchers and the activities of organisations such as the Together Pan. This has resulted in new monuments being erected and additional information being provided at existing monuments and sites specifically focusing on Holocaust memory. However, there is still some way to go before this network of sites is as well developed as it is in Poland for example. A new museum has just been opened at Sobibor, the Sobibor memorial is currently undergoing renovation and work is currently well advanced for the opening of a Warsaw Ghetto Uprising Museum planned for late 2025. Once open, this Museum will go some way to establishing parity with the more famous Warsaw

Uprising Museum that opened in 2004. By contrast there is little specific focus on the Holocaust in the Belarusian State Museum of the History of the Great Patriotic War.

The diverse elements of this historical context and the lack of access to information mean that Holocaust education, both formal and in the form of published accounts from Western historians have focused overwhelmingly on Auschwitz and to a lesser extent on the Warsaw Ghetto and the Operation Reinhardt Death Camps such as Chelmno, Sobibor, Belzec and Treblinka in Nazi occupied Eastern Poland. There is little doubt that events in these camps were beyond horrific, but they predominantly involved groups of Jews being transported there from elsewhere, often Western Europe, to be murdered, usually in purpose-built gas chambers. The Holocaust in the Soviet Union focused primarily, but not exclusively, on local Jews who were often shot in or close to their places of origin or residence. The German invasion of the Soviet Union started on 22nd June 1941 during Operation Barbarossa and progressed swiftly across the Western Soviet Union including Belarus with Minsk being occupied by the Nazis shortly after. The advance of the Panzer Divisions and the Wehrmacht was quickly followed by the advance of the Einsatzgruppen or mobile killing squads. These groups played a central role in some of the most notorious mass-murders of the Holocaust in the East such as Babi Yar, outside Kiev, and Rumbula and Bikernieki forests, outside Riga. Einsatzgruppe B was responsible for Belarus and parts of Western Russia and played a central role in the Holocaust in Belarus.

The Holocaust in Belarus

The Germans quickly established ghettos in many towns and cities throughout Belarus. These ghettos were extremely diverse in terms of size, geography, and experiences. There were not only significant differences between ghettos in countries such as Belarus, Poland, Latvia, Lithuania, and Ukraine, but also within individual countries. The ghettos in Warsaw and Lodz were the largest in Eastern Europe, with estimates of 400,000-500,000 and 150,000 prisoners respectively at their height. The barbarity of the Holocaust in Belarus is partially hidden due to the scale of the losses. Although estimates vary and accurate figures will never be known with certainty, Walke (2015) estimates that 800,000 Belarusian Jews were murdered in the Holocaust, between 80-90% of the pre-war Jewish population. It is impossible to begin to comprehend the Holocaust without some knowledge of the Holocaust in the East.

According to the Soviet census of 1939 the total population of Minsk was approximately 239,000. Anna Machiz estimates that approximately 75,000 Jews remained in Minsk at the time of the Nazi occupation with an estimated 100,000 prisoners in the Minsk Ghetto at its height after Jews were transported there from Germany and other parts of Europe as well as elsewhere in Belarus. At the other end of the scale there were numerous smaller ghettos with a few hundred or few thousand prisoners in towns and villages across the country.

I was lucky enough to have the opportunity to explore Jewish Rechitsa, a town 275km to the south-east of Minsk, which like many other places in Belarus had a century's old history of a large Jewish community. Kaganovitch (2013) estimates that a quarter of the 1939 population of Rechitsa (approximately 30,000) were Jewish although precious few traces of this rich history and heritage can be found in the modern town[4]. Estimates for the numbers of Jews murdered in Rechitsa, which did have a small ghetto, vary between approximately 1400 (Kaganovitch, 2013) and 3000 (Smilovistsky, n.d.). Other killing sites and ghettos in Eastern Belarus existed in the cities of Mogilev (estimated 10,000 Holocaust victims) and Gomel (estimated 3000-4000 victims). The location of Rechitsa, Mogilev and Gomel in Eastern Belarus meant that they were occupied slightly later by the Nazis than Minsk, allowing a significant proportion of the Jewish population to flee eastwards into the Russian interior. The speed with which Minsk was occupied, within days of the start of the invasion, meant that not as many Minsk Jews had the same opportunity. The establishment of the Minsk Ghetto was equally swift under a decree dated 19th July 1941[5].

The diversity of the characteristics of the numerous ghettos in Belarus, Eastern Europe and the occupied Soviet Union means that sweeping generalisations should be avoided. The archetypal image of a Nazi ghetto in Western eyes predominantly relates to the Warsaw Ghetto via photographs and film footage showing high walls and bridges between the small and large ghettos. These diverse characteristics mean that the experiences of ghetto prisoners were also different, making local analysis of the specific context of each place essential to understanding the overall horror of the Holocaust in the East, referred to as the "epicentre of the Holocaust" by Wade-Beorn (2018).

The specifics of the Minsk Ghetto

So, what are the specific characteristics of the Minsk Ghetto, the combination of which make both the Minsk Ghetto and the experiences of the Jewish prisoners there unique? The Minsk Ghetto in contrast to the Warsaw Ghetto was more porous, being surrounded by barbed wire rather than a high wall. This made it slightly easier (albeit still incredibly dangerous) for Jews to

---

[4] This is the same for numerous former Jewish communities in towns and villages across Belarus.
[5] See Order from the Field Commandant's office to create a Ghetto in Minsk in Section 3.

leave the ghetto in search of food and other essential supplies. Walke (2015) explains how this dangerous task was often undertaken by children as it was easier for them to escape unnoticed under the fence, a resource later harnessed by both the Jewish Ghetto Resistance and the Partisans to guide groups between the ghetto and the forests. The Minsk Ghetto was also the longest lasting of the large ghettos in the occupied Soviet Union (between July 1941 and October 1943). In combination with the relatively harmonious pre-war relations between the Jewish and non-Jewish populations, this provided opportunities for more intense interactions between the ghetto and the so-called Russian District of the city.

These interactions were essential to survival in the Minsk Ghetto offering an opportunity to trade in exchange for food with the non-Jewish population, who in turn had the freedom to travel to peasants in surrounding rural areas to trade goods received from the Jews for more food. These interactions often relied on pre-war contacts although the nature of the circumstances meant that such relationships and interactions were fraught with danger. The constant mortal danger of life in the Ghetto meant that old relationships changed, new ones were forged and there was a constant need for Jews of all ages in the ghetto to continuously adopt new survival strategies and roles. The role of individuals was in constant flux, gender roles were often reversed, and children often had to take on the roles of adults when parents, relatives and guardians were murdered.

The close proximity of dense forests around Minsk provided ideal conditions for Partisan activities and extensive movements of arms, food, medical supplies and people between the Ghetto Resistance and the Partisans. These interactions were also facilitated by the shared Soviet identity between the communist Partisans in the forests around Minsk and the (predominantly communist) Jewish Resistance in the Minsk Ghetto. Anna Machiz talks in detail about the nature and extent of these interactions and there is no doubt about their importance in terms of people escaping the ghetto and supplies being transferred between the ghetto and the Partisans. The proportion of Jews that escaped from the Minsk Ghetto is relatively high in comparison to other large ghettos due to the proximity of the forests, the porous nature of the ghetto and the co-operation between the Ghetto Resistance and the Partisans. However, many of these people were killed during the escape, on their way to the forests or in subsequent activities once they joined the Partisans (Kagan and Cohen 1998). The stories of many escapees will therefore never be told.

Most of the large ghettos in Eastern Europe functioned as transit camps where victims waited to be transferred to death camps for extermination. Although other ghettos witnessed killings, the Minsk Ghetto was the final destination for many Jewish victims murdered in regular pogroms where victims were shot or burnt in the ghetto itself, killing sites in close proximity such as Drozdy, Blagovshchina, Koidanov, Trostenets and Tuchinka or murdered in mobile gas vans on the way to pre-prepared mass graves. The nature of the Minsk Ghetto in comparison to other camps is captured in the foreword to this book in a quote from survivor Frida Reizman:

"The Minsk Ghetto was a place of death. We were only murdered there."

The integration of Jews in pre-war Minsk meant that Jews lived all over the city, although there was a concentration in a district to the west of the Svisloch River that dissects the city, an area Epstein (2008) refers to as the old Jewish neighbourhood. This area, to the north of Nemiga Street and adjacent to the Jewish Cemetery became the ghetto and although it was then on the fringes of the city centre, the district has since been consumed by the city centre and like the rest of Minsk is now unrecognisable due to post-war reconstruction. In contrast to the adjacent city centre dominated by brick and concrete buildings of several stories, the ghetto at the time retained much of the character of the former villages that surrounded Minsk in earlier times consisting of single-story timber constructions and a maze of streets and alleyways.

The limited extent of English language publications focusing specifically on the tragedy of the Minsk Ghetto coupled with the limited knowledge of Belarus and the horrors of the Eastern front amplify the importance of the story of Anna Machiz and supplement the valuable testimonies of survivors published in Bronstein and Demby (2018), the first book translated by the Together Plan, 'We Remember Lest the World Forget'[6]. The power of these narratives comes through strongly because of their vivid and personal nature. Clearly people experienced the Minsk Ghetto in different ways often related to gender, age, and pure luck. These personal insights into everyday life experiences explore issues in relation to life, loyalty, bravery, treachery and the life and death consequences of split-second decisions.

Narratives tend to reflect the character of the narrator and the raw and at times dry writing style of Anna, reflect her role as a Public Prosecutor in pre- and post-war Soviet Belarus. The fact that only 300 copies of the initial book 'We Remember Lest the World Forget' and 200 copies of Anna Machiz's memoirs were published in Russian further underscores the value and importance of these books in bringing these stories to a wider audience. The English language version of this book cements the place of the survivors in history, pays tribute to the

---

[6] See Preface by Debra Brunner.

memory of those who perished and informs an often-unfamiliar audience with the horrors that took place in Minsk. The lack of visible traces of the Minsk Ghetto further reinforces the importance of these accounts. Visitors to modern Minsk will require a guide to find traces of the Holocaust and the ghetto due to the almost complete reconstruction of the Hero City (one of twelve Hero City's designated in the Soviet Union after the War) and the lack of official recognition of the specific suffering of the Jews that characterised the post-war period. Anna's memoirs about the Minsk Ghetto can now take their rightful place in the historiography of the Holocaust and as part of 21st Century Holocaust discourse.

These stories need to be told.

Structure of the book

The origins and challenges of publishing this book are clearly outlined in the opening contributions by key players who have brought Anna's story to life, providing valuable contextual insights. The main body of the book is divided into three sections. Section 1 explores the history, memory and culture of the Minsk Ghetto and begins with an account by Anna's nephew and fellow survivor Leonid Tsyrinskiy without whom there would only have been 200 Russian language copies of the book in the world, many of which have undoubtedly been lost in subsequent years. The account explores his relationship with his mother and his aunt, Anna Machiz, and emphasises the importance of bringing Anna's writings, which were hidden in both State and family archives for so many years, to a wider audience. Hopefully this book will inspire researchers and families of descendants to search out new accounts and bring them to the attention of a wider audience in the same way that the 'We Remember Lest the World Forget' book seems to have inspired Leonid to bring Anna's story to the attention of the Together Plan.

There follows a brief account by Holocaust Educator Kuzma Kozak who further clarifies the journey that Anna's writings have taken from their origins in the Naliboki Forest to their eventual rediscovery, which led ultimately to this publication. The fact that the accounts were written by Anna shortly after the events and her escape to join the Partisans in Naliboki Forest strengthen the credibility and authenticity of her writings and make them all the more remarkable. Kuzma also provides an overview of various written documents about the Minsk Ghetto that have emerged and gained increasing interest since independence in Belarus in 1990.

The final part of Section 1 consists of an article by eminent historian Professor E. G. Ioffe that draws on a wide range of sources to provide valuable insights into not only Anna's activities in the Ghetto Resistance, but also her life and work before and after the War. The article finishes with the reproduction of various official documents confirming Anna's military exploits in various Partisan brigades including the Stalin and Zhukov battalions. The commentary elucidates the activities of Anna and the Partisan brigades she belonged to, some of the complexities of her post-war life in Soviet Belarus and contacts that she had with fellow Partisans in the post-war period. The contributions in Section 1 are powerful and in combination with the official documents reproduced and commented upon help to further consolidate the authenticity and credibility of her accounts.

Section 2 is undoubtedly the most important part of the book, the memoirs of Anna Machiz about the Minsk Ghetto. The first part of Section 2 contains the full account written by Anna in 1943, the second part is an appendix to the original memoirs and was written by Anna in 1981. The appendix provides a summary of the main text and is referred to by Professor Ioffe in his article in Section 1. Although this means some repetition, the inclusion of both the full version and the summary helps to reinforce the key messages. The main text is structured thematically, and the identified themes encapsulate the horrors of the content and the reality of life in the Minsk Ghetto. The themes explore the evolution of the Nazi atrocities in Minsk and the response of the Jewish Underground. The main account is signed "The Forest, A.S. Machiz, December 1943". No explanation required.

Section 3 reproduces some interesting supporting publications and documents that provide further background and facilitate a deeper understanding of Anna's memoirs. These are reproduced without commentary allowing the reader freedom to explore these historical sources. The first part of Section 3 reproduces writings by Anna in previous publications and a short extract from the appendix to Anna's memoirs. The final publication is an interview with Leonid Tsyrinskiy for a Belarusian newspaper in 2011 and focuses on Leonid's mother (Anna's sister), which contextualises the hardships his mother faced during the War. The interview also highlights the complexities of the lives of Ghetto survivors living in post-War Soviet Belarus. The lack of recognition of the specific suffering of the Jews in the Soviet official narrative meant that Ghetto survivors generally suffered in silence and the topic remained taboo. Monuments generally eschewed explicit mention of Jews, referring only to Soviet citizens. The Soviet narrative focused exclusively on the glorious victory of the Red Army and the suffering of the Soviet people, with no room for the specific suffering of the Jews. This situation continued until the post-Soviet period during which stories and memoirs have started to emerge and researchers have gained access to some Soviet archival sources to supplement archival sources in other countries.

Testimonies of Tragedy and Resistance in the Minsk Ghetto

The final part of Section 3 reproduces extracts from a range of documents, the majority written by different parts of the Nazi administration and security organs and focusing on aspects relating to the establishment and running of the Minsk Ghetto. These are again reproduced without commentary and allow the reader to reflect on the unimpassioned and mundane language used when considering the horrors of the subject matter. The adopted language style reflects the mentality of the Nazi administration, reporting on the mass-murder and genocide of the Jews as if they were requesting raw materials for a factory or stationery for an office. These insights further deepen our understanding of the horrors and the scale of the inhumanity encapsulated in the Nazi regime. The final document is from the Soviet authorities dated 1944 and focuses on the exploration of a mass-burial site on the outskirts of Minsk. This provides a glimpse of the aftermath once the Nazis had been expelled and has a power all of its own.

The remainder of the book contains a glossary of people, places, dates, and terms that will be useful to an English-speaking audience unfamiliar with the Soviet and Belarusian context. The final section contains a number of photographs and documents relating to Anna and various colleagues and family members including her nephew Leonid at different times before, during and after the War and a selection of fellow prisoners of the Minsk Ghetto. There are also a number of photographs of the original memoirs typed by Anna in the Naliboki Forest. These help to bring the story to life and to reinforce not only the collective tragedy of the Jews in the Minsk Ghetto, but also the very personal and individual nature of this tragedy.

Neil Adams,
Senior Lecturer Spatial Planning,
London South Bank University,
London, UK

My interest in the history of the Soviet Union and Central and Eastern Europe dates back to my work as a planning consultant and later an academic working on regional development projects primarily in the Baltic States and Poland from the mid-1990s onwards. I became particularly interested in the War and Holocaust history and became increasingly intrigued by this mysterious country called Belarus. Subsequently I spent a few summers volunteering with Chernobyl Childrens Project (UK) with children from an orphanage in Rechitsa, south-east Belarus and also spent holidays exploring War and Holocaust history, which is how I came into contact with the Together Plan. I knew immediately that I wanted to support their work and feel privileged to have been asked to make a contribution to this hugely important book. I hope that it helps to facilitate a deeper understanding of the Belarusian context within which Anna's story is situated for readers who have not been fortunate enough to explore the country and its history themselves.

Literature and Sources

1. Arad, Y. (2009), The Holocaust in the Soviet Union, Lincoln: University of Nebraska Press

2. Bronstein, H. and Demby, B. (2018), We Remember Lest the World Forget: Memories of the Minsk Ghetto, New York: JewishGen

3. Epstein, B. (2008), The Minsk Ghetto 1941-1943: Jewish Resistance and Soviet Internationalism, Los Angeles: University of California Press

4. Kagan, J. and Cohen, D. (1998), Surviving the Holocaust with the Russian Jewish Partisans, London: Vallentine Mitchell

5. *Kaganovitch. A. (2013), The Long Life and Swift Death of Jewish Rechitsa: a community in Belarus 1625-2000, University of Wisconsin Press*

6. Smilovistsky, L. (n.d.), Jewish Addresses in Rechitsa, Diaspora Research Institute of Tel Aviv University, available at https://www.jewishgen.org/Belarus/newsletters/mogilev/RechitsaLink/Rechista.pdf accessed July 2023

7. Wade-Beorn, W. (2018), The Holocaust in Eastern Europe: at the Epicenter of the Final Solution, London: Bloomsbury Academic

8. Walke, A. (2015), Pioneers and Partisans: An Oral History of Nazi Genocide in Belorussia, Oxford: Oxford University Press

9. Беларуская энцыклапедыя імя Петруся Броўкі (2019), Khatyn: Tragedy of the Belarussian People

Dedicated to

**my dear aunt Anna Semyonovna Machiz
(18.12.1910 – 28.08.1988)**

**and to my mother Anna Isaakovna Tsyrinskaya
(20.09.1914 – 27.11.1987)**

Minsk, 2011

Section 1

The Minsk Ghetto: history, memory, culture

Repaying a Debt
Leonid Tsyrinskiy, Minsk, September 2011

This small book is a tribute to two women who are close to my heart: my dear aunt Nyura (Anna Semyonovna Machiz) and her cousin (my mother) – Anna Isaakovna Tsyrinskaya. Both of them lived hard lives. Although fate took them in different directions, they never lost touch with one another. My mother was born in September 1914. In 1915 her father Isaac Kugel died fighting in the First World War. From 1916 onwards my mother lived with her cousin, Anna Machiz, and her family right up to the time when she herself married in 1934. In 1935 my sister, Sofya Tsyrinskaya, was born, and on the 16th of May 1941 so was I. At the time of my birth, my family lived in Rudensk, an urban settlement. My father, Abram Yefimovich Tsyrinskiy, was the director at the office of *Zagotskot*[7] and my mother was a housewife.

When the Great Patriotic War (WWII) began my family could not be evacuated immediately as my father had to move the livestock away from the border first, and only then see to his own fate and the fate of his family. Unfortunately, he never had the chance, as Rudensk was seized by the Nazis too soon. My father was forced into hiding. In December 1941 a traitor blew his cover, and my father was shot by a firing squad in the village of Titva.

My mother, with two small children (myself and my sister) found herself in the Rudensk Ghetto at the end of August 1941. Her husband's sister Dora Frid was there too, along with her three-year-old son Leonid. At the end of September 1941, just before the pogrom which took place on the 10th of October that same year, she[8] managed to escape the ghetto with Dora and all three children.

They made their way to Minsk, where they found themselves in the ghetto once more. They lived in hiding on Shornaya Street until mid-January 1942. They managed to escape the ghetto using German passports which Anna[9] helped them to obtain. They made their way to the village of Valoki near Radoshkovichi and lived in hiding in Valoki until July 1944.

---

[7] Russian: short for *Zagotovka skota* – livestock procurement. This was the name given to regional authorities which oversaw state supplies of cattle and swine to meat processing plants. Each region had its own.

[8] Leonid's mother.

[9] Leonid's aunt.

After the war Anna searched us out and from then on never left us unattended. She would always support us in whatever way she was able. From April 1974, after the death of her husband, Isaac Naumovich Levin, my family lived in the same flat as Anna until the final days of her life. She was a very honest, proper, and modest person, and a competent lawyer. She never talked about her past. I knew she was acquainted with the writers Vasily Grossman, Ilya Ehrenburg, and David Guy, and was friends with Grigory Smolar, with whom she kept up a correspondence after he left the USSR and with Rosa Lipskaya, Sarah Levina, Naum Feldman, and Aron Fiterson. At the time no-one in our family knew that they were previously members of the underground in the ghetto from 1941 to 1943 or knew of her exploits or testimony.

I will never forget Anna Semyonovna's kindness and care. To my sister and I she was a second mother. I am proud to publish her memoir of this time and give voice to this brave and principled woman, who cared for so many.

The tragedy of the Minsk Ghetto: the first testimonies of Anna Machiz, an inmate, partisan and member of the underground

Kuzma Kozak,
(Holocaust Educator, Minsk), 2010

Perceptions of the portrayal of the Minsk Ghetto.

How the Minsk Ghetto is portrayed depends to a great extent on how the tragedy is remembered or was experienced. Witnesses and historians give different accounts of the deaths of around 80,000 Jews. Their stories have much in common, but differences in aspects of these narratives result from the fact that people's experiences varied, or their memories of the events are already fading[10]. Anna Machiz's writings about the tragedy of the Minsk Ghetto are an example of this: for her they are given significance as the main event in her experience in the history of the Great Patriotic War. This was a time that brought interminable pain to the lives of millions of people brought about by the events which she saw and felt and which she logged during that tragic year of 1943. It was the year of the liquidation of the Jews of Minsk and those deported from other parts of Europe, and the year when the last surviving prisoners were those who had made it to safety amongst the partisans and members of the underground.

It was here that those survivors were able to fulfil their objective to fight Nazism to its destruction. Nazism was their mortal enemy and had to be destroyed. That is why, after their struggle to stay alive in the ghetto, what they wrote down takes on a somewhat different meaning to the accounts of others. There was no confusion or lack of clear purpose, only a hope and belief that victory would come and that their losses would not have been in vain. These are the words of victors, but within them the enormity of the uncertainty, fear, and treachery they faced, and the bereavement from the loss of relatives and loved ones can still be detected.

Anna Machiz's account constitutes some of the first words to be written about the Minsk Ghetto, penned in 1943 and repeated in later interviews. They

---

[10] This thought is not very clearly expressed. Kuzma Kozak may be suggesting that mainstream war memory in Belarus and Russia misrepresents the Holocaust; certainly, the Jewish Museum in Moscow pays more attention to Soviet Jews who participated in the war effort than to the extermination of the Jews by the Nazis.

were to be repeated by great public commentators, historians, and even eyewitnesses of the events in their own narratives about the tragedy, although these others did not always cite their source. After the War Anna Machiz's texts came to rest in the files of the KGB in the Central Party Archive of the Communist Party of Belarus. They have been cited by historians from Germany, Israel, America, and Belarus, but only now will one of the original texts be published.

The history of its creation and preservation is fascinating. It initially appeared in a *partisan detachment* and was then re-written for the NKVD's archive and was kept in the Party and state archives under restriction. But after Anna Machiz's death, one of the copies of the texts remained in the attentive care of her nephew Leonid Tsyrinskiy. The demand for important information, the appearance of the memories and documentary materials of former inmates of the Minsk Ghetto in print, and their analysis amongst historians generated interest. After 2008, a rise in demand from official state bodies, especially in the Republic of Belarus's educational system, for examples of the struggles and survival of prisoners of the ghetto that could be used in the task of educating younger generations, promoting intergenerational dialogue and the dialogue between yesterday's allied and enemy states, gained momentum. All of these things created an appetite for producing documents which the public could read. To this end, an evening dedicated to Anna Machiz's centenary was held in the Historical Workshop in Minsk in 2010.

Among the participants were historians and public figures from Belarus and Germany. The interest that was generated by reading these little-known documents about the Minsk Ghetto, and in translating the text into German with the help of students of the Minsk State Linguistic University, is in itself a contribution to intercultural communication.

"Avengers of the Ghetto", a book by Hersh Smolar, came out directly after the war in 1947.[11] It focussed attention on the traditional character of war: the resistance of the prisoners, the struggle of the Jewish partisans and members of the underground. Simultaneously to this, what was perhaps the first civilians' association for former prisoners of the Minsk Ghetto was being formed on the

---

[11] *Smolar H.* Ghetto Avengers. Minsk, 1947; *Smolar H.* The Minsk Ghetto. Soviet-Jewish Partisans Against the Nazis. Minsk, 2002; *Smolar H.* The Minsk Ghetto. Soviet-Jewish Partisans Against the Nazis. New York, 1989.

historical site of *Yama* (The Pit) where a mass killing of Jews was organised by the Nazis on the 2nd of March 1942.

Photo: From The Together Plan collection, added to the original text during editing. The Yama (Pit) Memorial, Minsk. Bronze sculpture 'The Last Way,' by architect Leonid Levin and sculptors Elsa Pollak and Alexander Finski, courtesy of the Republic of Belarus.

With the rise of state antisemitism, however, these people with their collective memories adopted a policy of silence. It was only in the 1990s after political change had taken effect in Belarus that the few surviving witnesses of the catastrophe felt their shared memory of the Holocaust could be aired. To begin with, it was historians and their accounts that set the framework for how the Holocaust was depicted[12]. Then this was extended by the testimonies of Mikhail Treister, Abram Rubenchik, Boris Chaimovich, Israel Lapidus – former inmates of the Minsk Ghetto – about the nature of the resistance[13], and those of

---

[12] *Kupreeva G.* The Minsk Ghetto. Hidden Truth // The Belarusian Past. 1993. No.2. p. 46-51; compiled by *R. Chernoglazova*. Minsk, 1999; *Ioffe E.* Belarusian Jews: Tragedy and Heroism: 1941-1945. Minsk, 2003; The Minsk Ghetto 1941-1943. Tragedy. Heroism. Memory / edited by *V. Balakirov, K. Kozak* / International Scientific Conference Proceedings, Minsk, 24 October 2003, Minsk, 2003; *Hecker K.* German Jews in the Minsk Ghetto / edited by *K. Kozak*; translated by *G. Skakun*. Minsk, 2007.

[13] *Galburt A.* Hell Survivor. Unforgettable. Minsk, 2003; *Rodzinskiy G.* Children of the Ghetto. Tel Aviv, 2004; Known "Unknown": Collection of Materials / compiled and edited by *Y. Basin*. Minsk, 2007; *Traister M.* Memory Glimpses. Memories, Thoughts, Publications. Schimmer vom Gedächtnis… Erinnerungen, Überlegungen und Publikationen / edited by *K. Kozak*. No.4. Minsk, 2007; Jewish resistance to Nazism in Belarus during the Great Patriotic War, 1941-1944 / compiled by *K. Kozak*. Minsk, 2010; *Epstein B.* The Minsk

Galina Davydova, Sima Margolina, Maya Krapina and others about survival in a time of mass murder[14]. Side by side with these accounts, documents and materials from family archives began to show signs of life. Amongst them were the documented memories of daughter and mother Klara (Leli) and Berta Bruk, Rakhil Rapoport, Berta Melomed and Khasya Pruslina[15]. The total collected memories about the tragedy of the Jewish people of Belarus also include passages published in the USA and Israel[16]. There are also two modestly sized books from Germany – brushstrokes painted by foreign witnesses on the canvas of memories about the tragedy of the Minsk Ghetto[17]. Nevertheless, in comparison to the sheer scale of the crime committed, very little has been left to us to enable us to preserve and keep the memories of the tragedy of the Minsk Ghetto and its history alive.

Ghetto 1941-1943: Jewish resistance and Soviet internationalism, University of California Press, 2008.

[14] *Davydova G.* From Minsk to La Manche or by the Roads of the Holocaust: Documentary Narrative. 2nd edition. Minsk, 2001; Alive... Yes, I am alive! The Minsk Ghetto in Memoirs by Maya Krapina and Frida Reizman: Materials and Documents / compiled by *M. Krapina, F. Reizman*; edited by *K. Kozak.* No.2. Minsk, 2005; *Zavolner G.* Life Given by Fate. A Book of Memoirs by a Former Prisoner of the Minsk Ghetto. Minsk, 2004; *Zavolner G., Galperina R.* Saved from Hell. Life and Destiny. / Edited by *K. Kozak.* No.1. Minsk, 2004; *Zavolner G., Kaplinsky S.* Lines Written by Destiny. Minsk, 2007; *Krasnoperko G.* Letters from My Memory. Minsk, 1984; *Levina-Krapina M.* Thrice-born. Memories of a Former Prisoner of the Minsk Ghetto. Minsk, 2008; *Margolina S.* Staying alive. Minsk, 1997; *Margolina S.* Staying alive. Minsk, 2010; *Croz V., Chauskaya-Ilyashova Z.* Forever Remembered: The Minsk Ghetto - Life, Tears and Love... / edited by *K. Kozak.* No.6. Minsk, 2007; *Krasnoperko A.* Briefe meiner Erinnerung. Mein Überleben im jüdischen Ghetto von Minsk 1941/42. Haus Villigst, 1991.

[15] Archive of Hasya Pruslina: Minsk Ghetto, Anti-Fascist Underground, Repatriation of Children from Germany / compiled by *Z. Nikodimova*; edited by *K. Kozak.* Minsk, 2010; Surviving is a Feat: Memories and Documents about the Minsk Ghetto / foreword, compiled by *I. Gerasimova, V. Selemenev.* Minsk, 2008; When Words Cry: The Diaries of Lyalya and Bertha Brook / preface by *L. Levin*; foreword, edited by *I. Gerasimova.* Minsk, 2004; Wenn Worte schreien und weinen. Tagebücher der Ljalja und Berta Bruk. Dortmund, 2008.

[16] *Rubenchik A.* The Truth about the Minsk Ghetto: The Documentary Narrative of a Ghetto Prisoner and Young Partisan. Tel Aviv, 1999; *Gavi J.* Young hero of the Minsk Ghetto. Paducah, 2000.

[17] *Loewenstein K.* Minsk, im Lager der deutschen Juden. Bonn, 1961; *Rosenberg H.* Jahre des Schreckens... und ich blieb übrig, das ich Dir's ansage. Göttingen, 1985.

Overcoming the past through memory.

The portrayal of the Minsk Ghetto is therefore familiar to us only via a small number of documentary contributions. It is one of the most tragic in Europe. However, it is poorly represented when it comes to surnames, faces in pictures, written recollections, and preserved documents. For a long time, no-one collected these, and the number of surviving witnesses of the tragedy and struggle of the Minsk Ghetto dwindled to little more than a hundred. Historians busied themselves studying other topics, leaving an information gap behind them when it came to this. Two attempts (in 2008 and 2010) by Sergey Tukalo, a postgraduate from the Belarusian State University (BSU), to overcome the barrier of mistrust that existed in higher academic circles were both met with failure[18]. Likewise, when Gennady Vinnitsa, an Israeli academic, tried researching Holocaust history in the eastern regions of Belarus, he ended up having to abandon his hopes of being awarded a degree by the Supreme Certification Commission, the government agency which oversees the awarding of academic degrees equivalent to a PhD in most post-Soviet countries[19]. In historian's circles, questions currently outnumber answers. With the events now beyond living memory, there is no way to verify peoples' accounts.

The former Jewish cemetery in central Minsk is a physical example of this. Here, over five thousand victims from Belarus, Germany, Austria, and Czechoslovakia lie in four burial sites. As yet, these graves are not marked with surnames. The death-camp Trostenets, where most of the inhabitants of the ghetto and city of Minsk were taken to be killed, is equally poorly known. Likewise, history has few tales to tell about Drozdy, Masyukovschina, the SD camp on Shirokaya Street, and deportations of prisoners to Auschwitz, Majdanek and Treblinka. For the most part, the Minsk Ghetto is only paid attention thanks to historical descriptions of deportations of Jews to it from Europe. Almost all of them were killed, but some of their names have been restored, and gradually information about each victim is returning to Minsk from Hamburg, Bremen, Düsseldorf, Berlin, Cologne, Bonn, Essen, and Vienna.

---

[18] *Tukala S.* Jewish Genocide and Struggle in the Minsk Ghetto during the Great Patriotic War (July 1941 to October 1943). Author's abstract of the thesis for the degree of Candidate of Historical Sciences. Minsk, 2008; *Tukala S.* Jewish Genocide and Struggle in the Minsk Ghetto during the Great Patriotic War (July 1941 to October 1943). Author's abstract of the thesis for the degree of Candidate of Historical Sciences. Minsk, 2010.

[19] *Vinnitsa G.* Nazi policy of genocide against the Jewish population in eastern and central Belarus, 1941-1944. Author's abstract of the thesis for the degree of Candidate of Historical Sciences. Minsk, 2008; *Vinnitsa G.* Holocaust in the occupied territory of eastern Belarus, 1941-1944. Minsk, 2011.

Anna Machiz's book also approaches the theme through memory. It contains both vivid blocks of text detailing what people lived through, and deep sorrow at their losses. The events she recounts are already partially familiar, but her accounts do not always correspond to mainstream opinions about the character of the tragedy and the struggle against the Nazis. It may be for the author of this text, that the distinctive world of the partisans which she inhabits, forms her narrative about German fascism and allows her to convey to us precise information about members of the resistance. That is one of the advantages of this document. Finding contemporary portrayals of the living and those who were killed in the thick of wartime events – Emma Rodovaya, Yakov Kirkoyeshto, Mikhail Gebelev, Matvey Pruslin, Hersh Smolar, Khasya Pruslina and others – is uniquely meaningful for the history of the Holocaust.

This initiative by Leonid Tsyrinskiy's family – to retell the main events experienced by someone involved in the tragedy of the Minsk Ghetto, through their family archive – therefore deserves our truest gratitude and respect.

In 2011, Professor E. G. Ioffe, a Belarusian historian, wrote the following article about Anna Machiz -

'A Woman of Legend: Criminal Investigator for the NKVD of the BSSR and Chronicler of the Underground in the Minsk Ghetto'

2011 marked the 70th anniversary of the beginning of the Great Patriotic War and the 66th anniversary of the Great Victory over German Nazism. One of the figures who fought courageously against Nazism was a citizen of Minsk. Her name was Anna Machiz (Levina) (1910 – 1988).

The whole world knows about the "Black Book[20]." This book mourns the tragic fate of the millions of Jews who fell victim to a bloody genocide and brutal death, and who departed this life during the Great Patriotic War. The Soviet writers Vasily Grossman and Ilya Ehrenburg worked on its creation.

A History of the Minsk Ghetto, part of the Black Book, shocks its readers to their very core. It is based on material produced by Anna Machiz, Grechanik, L. Gleizer and P. M. Shapiro. It was prepared for print by Vasily Grossman. Anna Machiz's nephew, Leonid Tsyrinskiy set about analysing and comparing "A History of the Minsk Ghetto" to Anna's memoirs, which had been written on a typewriter and kept in the Central Archive of the KGB of the Republic of Belarus and the National Archive of the Republic of Belarus. The conclusion was drawn by Leonid that it was Anna's memoirs, written in December 1943 in the Naliboki Forest, that formed the substantive basis of "The History of the Minsk Ghetto".

On the basis of these memoirs Vasily Grossman is rightfully considered to be the first chronicler of the history of the Minsk Ghetto. His book was prepared for print earlier than H. Smolar's world-famous *Avengers of the Ghetto*.

To readers versed in the activity of the antifascist underground in the Minsk Ghetto the names of its leaders and active members will be familiar;

---

[20] *The Black Book of Soviet Jewry*, also known as *The Complete Black Book of Russian Jewry*, or simply the *Black Book*. A powerful document of the anti-Jewish atrocities perpetrated by the Nazis in eastern Europe, as well as the activities of Jewish members of resistance movements in occupied territories during World War II.

Mikhail Gebelev, Grigoriy Smolar, Yakov Kirkoyeshto, Natan Weinhaus, Matvey Pruslin, Grigoriy Rubin, Samuil Kazhdan, Abram Nalibokskiy, Naum Feldman, Rosa Lipskaya, Yenta Maizles, Zalman Okun, Mikhail Mirkin, Lev Gurevich (Gurvich), Mikhail Kagan, Hanan Gusinov, Naum Burshtyn (Bruskin), Abram Shlyakhtovich, Yevel Rolbin, Moisei Levin, Boris Khaimovich, Wulf Losik, Khasya Pruslina, Lev Kulik, Sarah Levina, Tsipa Botvinnik, Iosif Mindel, Emma Rodovaya and David Hertzig (Zhenka).

However, few people would know that between 1941 and 1943, Anna Machiz was also a part of this underground movement, which according to recent data numbered around 330 people. In addition to her activities in Minsk, after she fled from the ghetto, between 1943 and 1944, she played an active role in the partisan movement within Belarus.

Indeed, despite there being hundreds of works written after the end of the Great Patriotic War about the history of the Minsk Ghetto and the Belarusian Jewish partisans, both in Belarus and abroad, very little is known of Anna Machiz. What we do know is that she is mentioned in the book *The Minsk Antifascist Underground,* and Anna Semyonovna Machiz is also mentioned in the records of the National Archive of the Republic of Belarus's records with respect to the activities of the Minsk underground [1, p.163].

What, therefore, do we know about Anna Machiz?

To answer this question, in addition to these publications, we can turn to archived materials, particularly those stored in the National Archive. Here there are a few preserved items handwritten by Anna which have been acquired from the family archive of her nephew Leonid Tsyrinskiy. Tsyrinskiy also preserved the memories of people who knew Anna closely and moved in the same circles as she did. And there are official records of her role before, during and after the War. Together, these materials provide a biography of this brave and resourceful woman.

Anna Semyonovna Machiz (Levina) was born on the 18th of December 1910 in Minsk to the family of a railway worker. Her father spent his whole life working in railway timber departments and died in 1932. Her mother was a housewife. After finishing secondary school, Anna Semyonovna was a technical worker, a clerk, and a secretary for the office of the Bobruisk Province Public Prosecutor between the 1st of July 1927 and the 28th of August 1928. In 1928 Anna began the first year of a degree in the Minsk Institute of Law (now the Faculty of Law, Belarusian State University) and graduated in 1931. From September 1931 until December 1932, she was an investigator for the public prosecutor's office of the Mozyr province. Anna wrote in her autobiography about the events of her life which immediately followed:

> "Sent to work in 1931 as an investigator in Mozyr, and from there, in connection with my husband's transfer to Leningrad, went with him there and worked as an investigator in the Narvskiy District of Leningrad (1932 – 1933).
>
> In 1933 returned to Minsk, where I worked as an investigator until 1941, that is until the beginning of the Great Patriotic War."

Anna's personal identification card identifies that from October 1933 to November 1936 she worked within the *militsiya* of the Belarusian SSR [BSSR] as an investigator in the criminal investigation of the NKVD of the BSSR and in 1936 was awarded with a watch bearing her name for good work ("For fighting crime").

In 1936 Anna was appointed as senior investigator of the Minsk Public Prosecutor's Office, and in March 1940 she became Investigator for Top-Priority Cases for the Public Prosecutor of the BSSR (later, this post was called 'Investigator for High-Priority Cases'). When the Great Patriotic War began, Anna was employed in this post. Looking at her biography during and following the war, her autobiography contains the following lines:

> "Tried to escape from Minsk on foot with mother, who was ill, but was captured by Nazis on occupied ground. In 1943 after my mother's death, I escaped to join the partisan detachment in the region of Baranovichi. Was in detachment No. 106 and in Zhukov brigade as combatant, Chief of Special Detachment and Deputy-in-Chief of Special Detachment of Brigade. After returning to Minsk recommenced my pre-war duties as Investigator for Top-Priority Cases for the Public Prosecutor of the BSSR. Worked until the end of 1945. Due to poor state of health filed an appeal to be released from duties in the Public Prosecutor's Office [sic]. Since October 1945, up to present, employed by Zorka newspaper [2]."

Anna Machiz,
between 1941 and 1945

This is the broad timeline of her biography, but it is the period of intense activity during the years of the Minsk Ghetto which is the focus of this book - the period from 1941 to 1945.

Attentive readers of Anna's memoirs written in 1943 in the Naliboki forest will conclude that she had undoubtedly featured amongst the members of the antifascist underground in the Minsk Ghetto in the years that preceded it. Such details and specifics of the formation and activities of the underground, especially in her memoirs of 1943, written before the release of H. Smolar's *Avengers of the Ghetto*, could only be known to one of its active members.

Objectively, therefore, we would be justified in concluding that Anna's memoirs of 1943 are one of the first sources providing contemporary insight into the history of the Minsk Ghetto. It includes a brief history of the ghetto's underground. Crucially, these events are revealed in chronological order providing an account of the progression of events.

In an addendum to her memoirs of 1981, it is identified that she was one of the leaders of the *desyatkas*[21], one of the 10 member organising groups for the resistance. *Desyatkas* were formed via personal connections and recommendations. Secretaries of the *desyatkas* were connected to the person with authority over their zone. There were four zones in total and the ghetto was one of them. The tenth member of the desyatka was the head and co-ordinator of the group and in the Minsk Ghetto the tenth member was identified as Rubenchik[22], although this name is missing from the list of leaders of underground groups active in the ghetto in Minsk in 1941-1944 [3, p.213-214].

The newer material in the *Addendum to the memoirs of Anna Semyonovna Machiz (Levina)*, which was an unpublished manuscript written on the 20th of November 1981 and kept in the family archive of her nephew Leonid also gives more insight of her experience and knowledge of the antifascist underground in the Minsk Ghetto, in particular the activities of Mikhail Gebelev and Grigory Smolar. Her interview with historian David Guy also provides a graphic account of her interactions with two people in the Minsk Ghetto against whom she had led cases and convicted while working in the BSSR's Office of the Public Prosecutor before the Great Patriotic War. One of them, Zyama Serebryanskiy, commander of the Jewish police in the ghetto, and the second, Monisov, a former cashier who was a regular inmate of the ghetto.

Having bumped into them both on the same day, the reaction of each to her was very different. Serebryanskiy, whilst working as part of the Jewish police had made contact with the communists and was supplying clothes and weapons to the partisans. He made contact and re-assured her and offered to help rather than seeking vengeance, whereas Monisov attempted to make trouble, searching her out and denouncing her to the Gestapo. She survived this betrayal as she had

---

[21] Desyatkas were literally groups of ten people, acting in cells.

[22] In the Black Book his name was misspelled as Rubenik.

registered with the *Judenrat* under a maiden name, whereas she was reported as Machiz, and was therefore missing from the records.

She commented that, "The ghetto was like that. Some people stay decent even while in mortal danger. Others, finding themselves at death's door, try to settle old scores. True, shared misfortunes bring people together, but they can also drive a wedge between them: one must look this unpleasant truth in the face. There are people who start to think only about saving their own skin, and the lower instincts come to the surface…" [5, p.178 – 179].

In 1942 Sofya Sadovskaya, an active member of the Minsk Ghetto underground, was the head of the Housing Department of the *Judenrat* for the ghetto. In a conversation with Leonid Tsyrinskiy, she spoke of the activity of the antifascist underground in the Minsk Ghetto. Anna Machiz's name came up in this conversation. At that point Leonid asked: "Was she a member of the underground?"

"Yes, she was," replied Sadovskaya.

After this Leonid asked a second question: "Why didn't you write anything about Anna in your memoirs, *Sparks in the Night*, published in 1970 in the book *Through Fire and Death*?"

Sofya Sadovskaya's immediate answer was: "I just forgot to". Then she added: "Sarah Levina can confirm that she was a member of the underground".

In 1992, Anna Pavlovna Kupreeva spoke about Anna Machiz's role in the activity of the antifascist Minsk underground. Kupreeva was one of the first researchers of the history of the Minsk Ghetto. She was a professional historian and Candidate of Historical Sciences, and a senior researcher at the History Institute of the Academy of Sciences of the BSSR (from 1979).

Documentary evidence

Documents held in the National Archive of the Republic of Belarus also allow us to trace Anna Semyonovna Machiz's military involvement. She became a partisan of the 106th Detachment in Stalin Battalion on the 4th of April 1943.

Then Machiz was transferred to the 25 Years of the *VLKSM* Detachment, G. K. Zhukov Battalion; part of the joint partisan forces of the Stolbtsy district in the region of Baranovichi.

In March 1944 Anna Semyonovna was appointed investigator for the Special Department of the brigade in that detachment. But in the official document this post was called "Representative of the Detachment's Special Department".

Below is a fragment of the document:

> Order to the USSR Marshal Zhukov Brigade
>
> *4th March 1944 No. 67*
>
> *Naliboki forest*
>
> I hereby appoint comrade Machiz Anna Semyonovna Representative of the Special Department, 25 Years of the *VLKSM* Detachment
>
> *Colonel Vasilevich, Commander of the USSR Marshal Zhukov Brigade*
>
> *Major Gaysarov, Commissar of the Brigade*
>
> *Captain Kaydalov, Chief of Staff of the Brigade*
>
> *Major Dudkovskiy, Chief of the Special Department of the Brigade*

[7, sheet 67]

Three months later a new order came through. Below is a fragment of this document:

> Order to the USSR Marshal Zhukov Brigade
>
> *12th June 1944 No. 93*
>
> *Naliboki forest*
>
> I hereby relieve the Representative of the Special Department of the 25 Years of the *VLKSM* Detachment Machiz Anna Semyonovna of her current duties and appoint her Deputy-in-Chief of the Special Department of the Brigade for Investigatory Matters.
>
> *Colonel Vasilevich, Commander of the USSR Marshal Zhukov Brigade*
>
> *Captain Kaydalov, Commissar of the Brigade*
>
> *Captain Bozhenko, Chief of Staff of the Brigade*

[8, l. 101]

What information do we have about the G. K. Zhukov Partisan Brigade, which was active in the region of Baranovichi?

This was one of the most effective partisan units in combat throughout the region. It carried out many successful operations against the German occupiers and their allies.

In February 1944 "the Zhukovites" destroyed 6 enemy freight trains and a bridge, and damaged the mechanical work stands in the depot of Minsk station. In March 1944, along with the *Komsomolets* partisan brigade, they routed an enemy garrison in the urban settlement of Mir, and in June-July destroyed the ford over the river Sulla, seizing 5 motor vehicles, a machine gun, 100 rifles and a baggage train, and took part in the "rail war" on the railway track between Negoreloe and Kolosovo.

In 1979 a memorial was placed in the village of Yeremichi in the Korelichi district in honour of G. K. Zhukov Brigade.

In 1953, responding to question 28 of her personal identification card application form "Did you take part in combat during the Civil or Patriotic Wars?" Anna Semyonovna wrote: "In combat with the partisans of the Zhukov Brigade" [8]. Dudkovskiy, Machiz and other members of the Special Department of the brigade had to fight a difficult and dangerous battle with the German Special Forces, especially the Abwehr, the security police and the SD.

When waging war against the partisan movement, the Nazis actively employed a network of agents, planting their secret helpers in the partisan detachments and amongst the local population. The Nazi Special Forces sent their agents into the partisan detachments pretending to be prisoners of war fleeing the camps or Jewish ghettos. They posed as deserters from the police or anti-Soviet military units, disguised as refugees, people who had lost their homes to fire, wandering beggars, civilians coming to the countryside to exchange their possessions for edible goods, or antifascist German soldiers who had decided to "come over" to the side of the partisans, not wanting to fight against the USSR.

These German spies and saboteurs set off to join the partisan detachments and brigades so that they could act to undermine them from within. They were given missions to gain the trust of the partisans and their commanders at any cost, gather information about where the partisan units were stationed, how many they numbered and their command structure, their armaments, supply points, tactics in battle, channels of communication with parts of the Red Army and the population, and partisan aerodromes.

Some of the agents had the mission of carrying out terror attacks (directed at the command and political structure of the detachments and brigades) and even carry out mass poisonings, inducing less-stalwart troops to commit desertion, looting and acts of violence against the population, thereby discrediting the partisan movement.

The National Archive of the Republic of Belarus housed a notification form sent on the 30th of April 1944. It was sent by the provincial leader of the Chekist operative group attached to the Baranovichi Region's Underground Party Committee, Colonel D. M. Armyaninov, to the chiefs of the special departments of the partisan brigades which made up the Baranovichi combined partisan forces.

Here are a few fragments of this form:

> The Minsk School of German Espionage, acting under the insignia of the UBY, on the 10th of April this year sent a number of their agents to the districts of Dzerzhinsk, Ivenets, Korelichi and others to carry out reconnaissance and sabotage missions. Further to this, on the 30th of April some 12 spies are to leave Minsk, 3 of whom will be men and 9 women. The women will be carrying medical supplies on their person – iodine, bandages – which are poisoned. There are two children travelling with them, taken from a children's home: a two or three-year-old boy and a two-year-old girl. These groups have been tasked to carry out sabotage missions. Take measures to detain them.

[9, sheet 46]

In 1961, while working in the Archive of the October Revolution and Socialist Construction in Minsk, Leonid happened to meet Colonel Rafael Lyudvigovich Vasilevich, former commander of the Zhukov Brigade of the joint partisan forces of Stolbtsy. A conversation ensued. Vasilevich began to discuss the feats of his brigade during the years of the Great Patriotic War. Leonid was interested in the activities undertaken by the German Special Forces against the partisans. As Leonid recalls, he mentioned two counterintelligence officers – Dudkovskiy and Machiz – thanks to whom several German spies were unmasked and arrested.

Anna Machiz's services in combat were acknowledged when she was awarded the Order of the Patriotic War 2nd Class and presented with medals titled "For a Partisan of the Patriotic War" second class and "For Victory over Germany in the Great Patriotic War of 1941-1945".

From the 1st of August 1944 Anna worked as an investigator for top-priority cases in the Office of the Public Prosecutor of the Belarusian SSR. On the 10th of October 1945 the official rank of Counsellor of Justice was conferred on her:

Excerpt from an Order of the Public Prosecutor of the
Union of the SSR [= USSR]

Moscow No. 1136

10th October 1944

On the basis of the Decree of the Praesidium of the Supreme Court of the USSR of 16/IX-43 [16th September 1943] "On the establishment of official ranks for investigators/prosecutors employed by bodies affiliated to the public procuracy" the following official ranks are to be conveyed:

Counsellor of justice

On Machiz Anna Semyonovna – investigator for top-priority cases of the Office of the Public Prosecutor of the BSSR

K. Gorshenin, Public Prosecutor of the Union of the SSR.

---

[10]

Anna Semyonovna bore the title of Lieutenant Colonel of Justice. Furthermore, she was awarded two certificates of honour by the Central Committee of the Belarusian Komsomol.

In many cases, the fact that Anna saw her duties as an investigator as lying outside her duties to the Party (as well as the fact that she was a Jew) did not suit the sensibilities of the Republic's leadership. We should not forget that the years of 1944-45 saw the first post-war wave of the antisemitic state policy which ran through the whole of the USSR, including the BSSR. Anna Semyonovna was perfectly aware of this and made no indication that during the War she had been located in the Minsk Ghetto. When answering questions about her location in the territories temporarily occupied by the Germans during the Patriotic War (where, when, and how she had been employed during this time) on her personal identification card, Machiz wrote "In Minsk. 1941-1942. Lived in hiding, illegally" [11] instead.

She understood that she would not be objectively and fairly allowed to continue working if her record was otherwise. On the 27th of September 1945 Machiz was let go from the Office of the Public Prosecutor of the Belarusian SSR:

Moscow No. 1136

10th October 1944

On the basis of the Decree of the Praesidium of the Supreme Court of the USSR of 16/IX-43 [16th September 1943] "On the establishment of official ranks for investigators/prosecutors employed by bodies affiliated to the public procuracy" the following official ranks are to be conveyed:

Counsellor of justice

On Machiz Anna Semyonovna – investigator for top-priority cases of the Office of the Public Prosecutor of the BSSR

K. Gorshenin, Public Prosecutor of the Union of the SSR.

---

[11]

Excerpt from an Order of the Public Prosecutor of the Belarusian SSR:

Minsk No. 129

26th September 1945

From 27th September 1945 Comrade Machiz Anna Semyonovna is to be relieved of her duties as Investigator for Top-Priority Cases in the Public Prosecutor of the BSSR and let go from the offices of the Public Prosecutor in accordance with a declaration made by her.

Public Prosecutor of the Belarusian SSR

State Counsellor of Justice, 2nd Class

(I. Vetrov)

---

[12]

It is true that in her own autobiography of 1953 Anna explained the reason for her release from the Office of the Public Prosecutor as "a poor state of health and inability to continue with operative work". From October 1945 onwards she worked as a literary professional at the head of the correspondence department of *Zorka*, a newspaper of the Republic, a lawyer in the Kirov machine-tool construction factory in Minsk, and in **Beltorgsnab,** **Bel**orusskoye **tor**govoye **snab**zhenie (Belarusian trade supplies), a government-owned wholesaler that provided shops in Belarus with goods.

At the annual meetings for partisans of the Zhukov Brigade, Anna Machiz came across Pyotr Vintkyevich Dudkovskiy (1917 – 1997) several times. He had been her companion-in-arms and simultaneously her "Chief". He was the former Chief of the Special Department and simultaneously the Deputy Commander of the Zhukov partisan brigade for intelligence and counterintelligence. After the partisan brigades and detachments had merged with the Red Army, he worked as a Deputy Public Prosecutor in the Baranovichi region, a Deputy, and First-Deputy Public Prosecutor for the Public Prosecutor's Office of the BSSR and simultaneously as the Head of Administration for Investigations of the Public Prosecutor's Office of the Republic. He offered Anna a job at her old workplace, but she turned it down.

In 1948 A. S. Machiz was chosen as a Deputy for the Stalin District Council of Workers' Deputies.

There is an interesting document kept in Leonid Tsyrinskiy's family archive. It reads as follows:

> *"Kirov machine-tool construction factory*   Reference
>
> This document is issued to Levina Anna Semyonovna to confirm that she did work as a lawyer at the Kirov Machine-Tool Construction Factory in Minsk from the 20th of February 1954 to the 14th of June 1958 and was released to take up a post in *Beltorgsnab*, for regularisation of her length of service record."

[13]

Anna Semyonovna Machiz passed away on 28th of August 1988 aged 77.

Despite certain gaps in our information about the life and activities of Anna Machiz, we would be justified in coming to the conclusion that she was an ardent patriot, an active member of the Minsk Ghetto underground, a courageous partisan, a skilful counter-intelligence agent, an objective, fair investigator and an interesting memoirist: a truly legendary woman.

Without Anna Machiz's memoirs it would be impossible to reconstruct a full, comprehensive history of the Minsk Ghetto today. Anna Semyonovna Machiz's whole life and her contributions make the memory of this remarkable woman worthy of an eternal place in our hearts.

Literature and Sources

10. Minsk Anti-Fascist Underground / compiled by *Y. Baranovsky* [and others]. – Minsk, 1995.

11. From the autobiography of A. S. Machiz, kept in the family archive of L. A. Tsyrinskiy.

12. Minsk Anti-Fascist Underground / compiled by *Y. Baranovsky* [and others]. – Minsk, 1995.

13. Addendum to the memoirs of Anna Semyonovna Machiz (Levina). – 20.11.1981

14. *Guy D.* The Tenth Circle: Novels / D. Guy – Minsk, 1991.

15. National Archive of the Republic of Belarus (henceforth: NARB). – F. [file] 1450. – Op. [special folder] 5. – D. [document] 397. – L. [sheet] 3.

16. NARB. – F. 1399. – Op. 1. – D. 557.

17. Idem

18. NARB. – F. 3500. – Op. 21. – D. 78.

19. From the family archive of L. A. Tsyrinskiy.

20. Idem

21. Idem

22. Idem

Section 2

The Minsk Ghetto
as remembered by Anna Machiz

In the dark ages of Tsarist Russia, the Jews underwent many trials over many years. In effect, they had no rights. Tsarism based its politics on the divide between nationalities. National minorities, of which the Jews were one, were oppressed. Antisemitism thrived and was practised by the Tsar's officials. Jews did not have the right to hold positions of responsibility, work in the civil service, hold an officer's rank in the army, practise agriculture or obtain land or forests as property.

The choice of professions available to members of national minorities was limited; only a certain number of Jews could be accepted into educational institutions, and their percentage in comparison to students of other nationalities was strictly regulated. The well-to-do section of the Jewish population filled leftover empty spaces in secondary educational institutions. For the most part, the bourgeoisie had their children educated abroad.

The city of Minsk was part of the Pale of Settlement. The Jewish poor settled on streets such as Nemiga, Staromyasnitskaya and Novomyasnitskaya, Zamkovaya, Zaslavskaya, Sukhaya, Novoromanskaya, Yevreyskaya (Russian for 'Jewish street'), Nizhniy Bazar Kalvariya, Komarovka and others (see map). On the whole, Jews settled next to each other depending on their type of occupation: this was in places where markets were created or wherever it was easiest to manufacture their goods and sell them off. During the Tsarist times Jews were not forbidden from settling across the whole city and were free to go to shows and visit institutions, trading houses, banks, and work sites.

When the Soviets came to power in 1917, the Jews breathed a sigh of relief. Like all the other peoples of the multinational Soviet Union, they were afforded full rights. The Jewish proletariat and intelligentsia gained unlimited access to participate in all aspects of ownership, scholarship, and art where they could put their abilities to use.

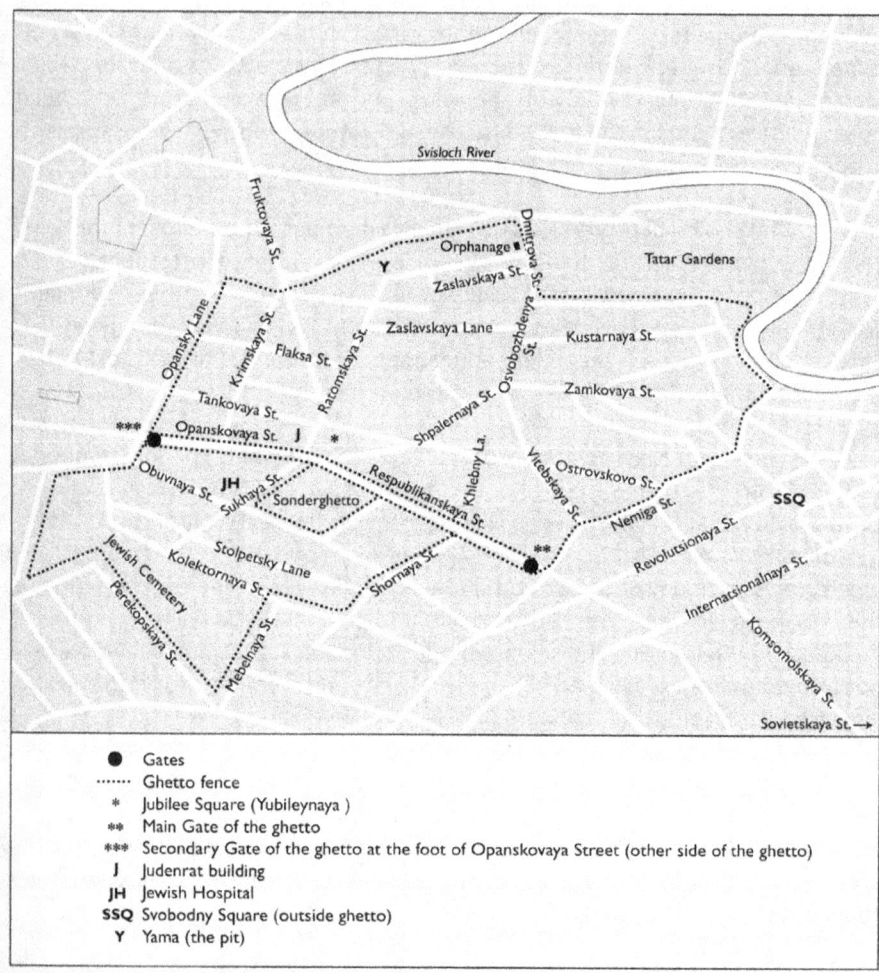

Map 1. The Minsk ghetto, showing original boundaries. Adapted from Dan Zhits, *Gito Minsk ve'Toldotav le'Or ha'Teud he'Xadash* (The History of the Minsk Ghetto in Light of the New Documentation), Basic Research Series no. 13 (Ramat-Gan: Bar Ilan University, 2000) 5; additional data from Abram Rubenchik, *Pravda o Minskom Geto* (The Truth about the Minsk Ghetto) (Tel Aviv: Krugozor [Prospect], 1999) 184–85.

Image: Map of the Minsk Ghetto.
Image attribution: Barbara Epstein, CC BY-SA 3.0 via Wikimedia Commons.

Testimonies of Tragedy and Resistance in the Minsk Ghetto

Jews gained the right to take up posts of command as equals with those of other nationalities, work in higher educational institutions and settle wherever they were able and saw fit to. The Jews gained their own homeland too[23]. The country thrived, along with all the different peoples living in it – the Jews included.

From the moment of its creation and throughout its history, the city of Minsk never saw a single ghetto until the arrival of fascist German invaders in 1941. On the 22nd of June 1941, the thunderclouds of war began rolling in. Germany had attacked the Soviet Union. By the 28th of June 1941 German soldiers were walking the streets of Minsk and the air was full of the rumble of German tanks. Around 75,000 Jews together with their children, who had missed their opportunity to leave, remained in Minsk. They were now seized by the German monsters.

From the very first day when the German wolfpack arrived in town, outrages began to be perpetrated: theft, violence, and executions at gunpoint for no reason at all. The Peaceful citizens of Minsk, especially the Jews, turned into objects to be degraded.

Early days of repression

The first decree issued by these fascist dogs informed the population of Minsk that the city was now 'free from the banditry of the Bolsheviks and yids' and ordered that all men between the ages of 15 and 45 report to a recruitment office, with the threat that non-compliers would be shot.

Hundreds and thousands of men turned up to the assembly point, obeying the German authorities' order. They were all sent off to a camp – Drozdy – where they were split up according to nationality. Russians and Jews were held separately from one another. They were starved, forbidden from using water from the river flowing nearby, beaten, and hit over the head with bottles. The Russians and Jews alike were subjected to degrading treatment and violence. The guards shot dead Soviet citizens for no reason at all, sometimes ten at a time, sometimes hundreds.

After some time, the Russian men were allowed to go, while the Jews were kept in the camp. Those who remained were divided into two groups:

---

[23] Machiz is probably referring to Jewish Autonomous Oblast: a region founded in 1928 in the far east of Russia on the border of China as a homeland for Soviet Jews. Incentives were created in the 1930s to entice Jews from the Soviet Union and abroad to settle there. (*Translator*)

intellectuals and physical labourers. The first group were loaded into carrier vehicles, driven out of town and shot dead with machine guns. All in all, over 3000 people were shot. Among those killed were distinguished figures such as senior lecturers in engineering at the polytechnic institute[24], Eisenburg and Prytykin, Candidates of Technological Sciences, Pryklad, a Doctor of Mathematical Sciences, and other academics who had trained hundreds of highly qualified people for the workforce.

The second group, consisting mostly of workers of various disciplines, were marched out of the camp and into town by a reinforced convoy and interned in jail. As they were led through the street's local residents, mostly women and children, ran outside trying to find people they knew or were related to among the crowd. But soon the streets emptied, and the meetings came to an end - because as people ran out to meet the convoy, the guards shot them on the spot. One column of people was taken down Kommunalnaya Street. A fourteen-year-old girl came running out of her block and stopped by the gates, hoping to catch sight of her father: then a shot rang out, and the girl dropped dead. Bunin's sister was shot right beside her - there were corpses lying all around. Almost every single house was overtaken with crying and confusion.

The workers spent several days in jail, after which some were released and sent to work for the Germans, while others were loaded into vehicles, driven out of town, and shot. That was how the Germans' henchmen dealt with the Jewish population.

Block No. 21 on Myasnikov Street was densely inhabited by more than 300 people. On the morning of the 2nd of July 1941, it was surrounded on all sides. The inhabitants - adults, the elderly and even children - were led out into the yard. A convoy numbering 40 people armed with rifles and handheld machine guns held these people at gunpoint for 6 hours. Hitler's evil men threatened to shoot these peaceful citizens if they so much as stirred from the spot. From time to time a shot would be fired to add realism: this made it seem as though the executions had begun. Meanwhile, a search was being conducted in their living accommodation. Under the pretence of looking for weaponry, they were being robbed: clothes, linen, blankets, footwear, crockery and even foodstuffs were taken. Like ravenous predators the fascists pounced on foods such as sugar, honey, butter, cacao, and rice. All these stolen goods were loaded onto two big carrier vehicles and taken away. Only after this was everyone allowed to go. Soviet citizens stared in disbelief at their ransacked living spaces,

---

[24] The Belarusian State Polytechnic Institute, now renamed the Belarusian National Technical University.

laughing despite themselves: "Hitler can't have been keeping his soldiers and officers well fed if they were that desperate to get at our food!"

On the 7th of July 1941, the German barbarians broke into people's accommodation and grabbed the first Jewish men they could lay their hands on – these men had just returned to the city – they put them in cars to be taken away. The next day a new decree was issued stating that 100 'communist yids' in Minsk and the surrounding region had been shot for having links with the Bolsheviks.

By night there were raids carried out by groups of four or five. They returned to homes belonging to Jews – the Graivors, the Rapoports and the Kleonskiys – and commanded them to turn over their remaining goods: "There were some silver spoons here, where's that suit, where did that silk get to?", the bandits shouted. If doors were not opened to these bandits, they would break them down.

On the same street – Myasnikov – there was a big building: the Stalin School. Its windows overlooked a yard below a residential block whose windows were placed in such a way that you could see the indoor areas of the residential block from the windows of the school. Having occupied the school, the Germans took to using the inhabitants of the block to amuse themselves and have some fun. Day and night they would take pot shots from their windows, hitting mirrors, furniture, and people.

Establishment of the Judenrat and the Ghetto

By decree of the German authorities the whole Jewish population was required to register to a specially created Jewish Committee (the Yids' Rade or *Judenrat*). The order included a warning that unregistered Jews would be refused accommodation in apartments in the upcoming resettlement.

The Jewish Committee was formed in the following manner: members of the Gestapo caught ten men on the streets, took them into the House of Government[25] and announced that they were now a Jewish Committee bound to carry out every order issued by the German authorities. If they committed the slightest offence, they would be shot. Ilya Mushkin, previously the Deputy Director of the Ministry of Industry and Trade, was elected Chairman of the Committee.

---

[25] The building which housed the Supreme Soviet of the BSSR, and one of the few to survive the war, still stands in Minsk today. It was designed by Iosif Langbard, an architect from a Jewish family.

By the 15th of July 1941 the registration of the Jews had been completed. By this date, all Jews were expected to start wearing yellow badges of a standard size on their chests and back, or else be shot. By the 31st of July 1941 the resettlement of the Jews had been completed. After the order concerning the yellow patches, another one was issued by the German authorities to create a ghetto. When they read this order, Soviet citizens couldn't believe that what they were seeing was a reality and not some fantasy or dream. Hitler was taking people from the 20th century, a century of high culture and technology, cars, aeroplanes, and the radio, and dragging them back into the depths of a past which had existed many hundreds of years before, to those centuries when Jews could only settle in certain allocated quarters of cities. These quarters were even called ghettos. Hitler was taking Soviet citizens back to the Middle Ages. On top of this, a war indemnity was to be levied from the Jews: gold, silver, and Soviet tender.

Driven out of their old familiar haunts in crowds, the Jews left their homes, furniture, and belongings, taking with them only the bare necessities. Having no means of transport, they had to carry their possessions with them on their shoulders. The standard living space allocated was 1.5 m^2 per person, not including children.

The process of resettlement was degrading enough in itself: a strictly demarcated district was created for the ghetto, but as soon as people began to move in, a new order would be issued, cancelling some areas, and adding other new ones. For ten days from 20th to 31st of July 1941 the Jews wandered about, migrating from one place to another.

By the 1st of August 1941, the resettlement of the Jews was complete. And so, the ghetto was created and included the following streets: Khlebnaya, Nemiga Lane, part of Respublikanskaya, part of Ostrovskaya, Yubileynaya Square, part of Obuvnaya, part of Shornaya, part of Kollektornaya, 2nd Opanskiy Lane, Fruktovaya, Tekhnicheskaya, Tankovaya, Krymskaya and others (see map on page 49). These streets were isolated from the centre of town and trading and industrial sites, but the Jewish cemetery in its entirety came within the bounds of the ghetto. The ghetto was surrounded by five lines of barbed wire. Anyone straying beyond this barbed wire would be shot. Anyone socialising with the local Russian population would also be shot. Trade and purchase of foodstuffs was forbidden to the Jews; anyone who disobeyed was to be shot. Execution at gunpoint became a constant companion to Jewish existence.

The Cherno family numbered six people: two adults and four young children. The husband was a labourer, and his wife Anna couldn't stand to see her hungry children suffer, and so she went to the Russian District to see if she could get some help from her friends. As she was returning home, she was stopped by policemen who took everything that was on her, brought her to jail and then had her shot. The same fate befell Rosalia Taubkina when she set foot across the barbed wire to meet with her Russian relatives.

Degradation, violence, and murder

No sooner was the ghetto surrounded by wire than the Jews began to be subjected to robberies and violence. At any time, day or night, the Germans would drive up to the ghetto in vehicles or come on foot. They would enter the places where the Jews were living and act as though they owned the place: they stole and took away with them anything they liked. These robberies were accompanied by beatings, degradation and often murders.

These feral bandits attacked Jewish homes by night and murdered their residents. The murders happened every night and in particularly brutal ways: eyes were gouged out, tongues and ears cut off, skulls smashed and so on. There was no authority to turn to in protest since the murders were organised by the Gestapo responsible for devising methods for exterminating the population.

The district encompassing Shevchenko, Zelyonaya, Zaslavskaya, Sanitarnaya, Shornaya and Kollektornaya streets was particularly hard hit. When they knew that their street was under attack, the Jews would reinforce their living spaces by installing a second set of doors behind the front doors, fitting iron bolts, not opening up when the bandits knocked at the door, setting up rotas for keeping watch and organising themselves for self-defence, but all this was useless against an armed enemy: doors and windows were simply broken down. One gang broke into the building where the doctor Zefir Margolina lived. They beat everyone up, murdered two and gravely wounded Margolina with four bullets. The Kaplan family, who lived on Zaslavskiy Lane, were subjected to long-lasting torment. The father had his eyes gouged out, the daughters had their ears cut off, and the other members of the family had their skulls smashed, after which they were all shot dead. The next morning neighbours said that the bandits had been wearing masks and spoke German.

At this time a wave of pogroms swept across all the ghettos in the BSSR. Jews were made to carry sand and clay from one site to another and back and to dig the soil without shovels. The "wage" which the Germans paid, for this and all other kinds of labour, consisted of 200 grams of bread and a watery concoction, which was given out once a day and infamously known as "German soup".

A member of the White Guard[26] was appointed to be commandant of the camp and simultaneously master of the ghetto. This animal was named Gorodetskiy and had sold out to the German fascists. Robberies, violence, and murders were his chief speciality.

One of the greatest experts in the BSSR: Professor Siterman, Doctor of Medical Sciences was left living in the city since he had not evacuated in time. As soon as Gorodetskiy and the Gestapo became aware of Siterman's existence, the Professor's ordeal of degradation began. Gorodetskiy broke into the building where Siterman was located demanding valuables. He took everything that he felt like taking and beat the scholar up. Agents of the Gestapo then turned up at Siterman's place and took him away. He was made to do hard, dirty labour clearing out cesspools and lavatories with his bare hands.

In October 1941 Siterman was given a shovel to hold and was made to stand in a lavatory for a photo. A few days later a passenger vehicle was sent to take him away. No-one ever saw the Professor again.

Removing the men from the ghetto

A large number of men were left in the ghetto. They were all registered with the Department of Labour of the Jewish Committee. Later on, this department received the title of 'the Labour Market'; from here, all men were sent, on demand, to do hard forced labour on military building sites, for businesses and at the Soviet prisoner of war work camp on Shirokaya Street.

On the 14th of August 1941, a rumour spread through the ghetto: "they're rounding up the men". Sure enough, part of the ghetto was surrounded, the men were loaded onto vehicles and driven away by the Gestapo. They explained that it was necessary to extract these men to work on military building sites, but what the Gestapo called "work" in every other language meant death.

On the 26th of August 1941 approaching 5 o'clock in the morning passenger vehicles appeared, racing towards the ghetto. Within five minutes the ghetto was surrounded. Out of these vehicles came agents of the Gestapo, who broke into buildings where the Jews were living, and like wild beasts they cried "männer!" ("men"). They forced all the men out onto Yubileynaya Square, beat them up, made a mockery of them and then drove them away.

---

[26] Anti-communist forces which had fought against the Bolsheviks during the Russian Civil War and continued to lead smaller armed insurrections against the Soviets until World War II.

On 31st of August 1941 the round-up was repeated. The ghetto was quickly surrounded by vehicles. This time not only men were taken, but also women who had somehow displeased the fascists for example because their yellow patches were not sewn on well enough. At the same time the Jewish buildings were raided.

The people removed during the raids of the 14th, 26th and 31st of August 1941 were taken to jail and shot - around 5000 people in total. The Jews lived in this way until the 7th of November 1941[27] expecting new horrors with every passing day.

Resistance

The aim of German fascism was to create a mental state of panic amongst the Jews, to infect their thoughts and actions, to plant the idea in people's consciousness that everything was lost for them and that there was no way out of the heavy chains of the fascist yoke. But Hitler's henchmen had made a mistake in their calculations: they had forgotten that they were dealing with Soviet Jews, Jews who had been living a full and free life for the last 28 years. They had forgotten that these Jews were raised with a fighting spirit and a thirst for victory.

From August 1941 a mustering of forces for an organised resistance to the enemy began. Those Jewish communists still left in the city of Minsk sought each other out and agreed to hold an Underground Party meeting. In block no. 54 on Ostrovskaya Street this group of communists gathered for the first time. Amongst them were: Weinhaus, a member of the Council of People's Commissars; Schnittman, Khaimovich and Feldman, workers at the Belostok textiles factory; and Smolar, a member of the Union of Soviet Writers. The meeting mandated the creation of an Underground Party organisation which set itself the following tasks:

1. Break the mental state of panic prevalent among the Jews created by the German fascist thugs.
2. Set up a radio receiver.
3. Initiate a system of leaflet distribution.
4. Initiate contact with the communists in the Russian District.
5. Establish links with the partisan detachments outside of the ghetto.

The first steps taken by the Underground Party organisation were met with success. The Germans issued an order to hand over all precious items – gold,

---

[27] 7th November was the date of the first major pogrom in the ghetto.

silver, and other valuables – to the German authorities. Meanwhile, the Underground Party group mandated for all these valuables to be redirected to the partisan detachments, and some of them were successfully delivered.

The Germans shouted to the whole world about their victories in the newspapers. Meanwhile, the Underground Party group took to systematically distributing leaflets which reflected the true state of affairs, showing the extent of the falsehoods about fascist victories and calling the Soviet people to arms.

These leaflets were read with great interest and passed from person to person. On meeting each other, instead of a greeting, people would ask: "Is there any news today?" (In Yiddish: "Es hert zikh epes nayes haynt?"). It was all you could hear from every direction. The Jews were always waiting for a new leaflet or communication. The leaflets themselves and written copies of them were passed from house to house. Weinhaus was appointed the editor of the leaflets.

On the 31st of September 1941 Kiriyeshto, one of the leaders of the Underground Party group in the ghetto, was murdered by the German monsters. His place in the Party leadership was taken by Gebelev, instructor of the Kaganovich Central Committee of the Party in Minsk. He was tasked with establishing contact with the communists in the Russian District. The possibility of convening a joint Underground Party conference was raised. Misha Gebelev was appointed to represent the Underground Party group of the ghetto when contacting the communists in the Russian District.

While Hitler's dogs tried to spread tension between different nationalities, the Jewish underground leader, Gebelev was risking his life to save Russian communists from German jail. He would go into the Russian District outside of the ghetto and seek out where his comrades were living and hiding Russian communists. He then brought some of them to the ghetto and hid them in *malinas*. Near the ghetto in the Russian (non-Jewish) district, reserve living spaces had been identified. Here communists from the non-Jewish Russian District and Jewish communists from the ghetto would plan out their actions together.

In September 1941 contact was established with the partisan detachment of Captain Bystrov in the East. It was this brigade that sent the first guides and received the first party of people from the ghetto: 20 people, most of whom were communists and combat-ready individuals: Schnittman, Khankovich, Gordon, Okun and others. The Underground Party group mandated that systematic help should be arranged for the partisan detachments in the form of warm clothes, basic possessions, soap, and salt.

Despite the Party group's appraisal of the Jewish Committee (the *Judenrat*) as an organ for enacting the occupational politics of the German authorities, they still considered it necessary to contact the Soviet elements within the *Judenrat*, using them as a means to help the partisan movement, as well as Jews and their families escaping to its detachments. First, contact was initiated with Mushkin, Chairman of the *Judenrat*. Then the head of the industrial sector of the *Judenrat* Ruditzer and the Chief of the Jewish police Serebryanskiy were brought on board to help the partisan movement. It was they who passed on basic provisions to the leaders of the partisan group for the partisan detachments: furs, footwear, linen, warm clothes, typewriters, stationery, soap, medical supplies, money and sometimes even foodstuffs such as salt.

The fascist jackals ran about through the ghetto, not giving Jewish households a moment's peace. Their attacks were to be expected at any moment, but all the same, despite this, Jewish women and even the elderly kept on helping the partisans, sewing them underwear and camouflage suits, and knitting socks for them, creeping down to their cellars at night with only slivers of light to see by. The ghetto's workshops, with Goldin at their head, were for the most part working for the partisans.

At this time the Jewish communists of the ghetto and the communists of the Russian District raised the possibility of a joint meeting to create a single Underground Party organisation for the city of Minsk. In September 1941 a preliminary meeting was held, but the attempt to convene a conference during this period failed due to the subsequent events. These were the first steps taken by the Underground Party in the ghetto.

Pogroms in the Ghetto

On the 6th of November 1941 a rumour spread that on the anniversary of the *October Revolution* there would be a pogrom in the ghetto[28]. Gorodetskiy arrived in the ghetto. He chose a group of workers and experts together with their families and gave the order for them all to be moved to the Soviet prisoner of war camp on Shirokaya Street. Some of the *Judenrat*'s members were relocated there too.

The 24th anniversary of the *October Revolution* was now drawing near. That anxious night, the Jews couldn't sleep. They sat and waited for the morning. As the first morning light appeared, big black vehicles with closed compartments

---

[28] The date of the October Revolution was 7th of November 1917 in the Gregorian calendar (25th of October 1917 in the old style, Julian calendar).

could already be seen entering the ghetto. The agents of the Gestapo were armed with whips, revolvers, and hand-held machine guns. With shouts, whistles, and maniacal laughter those monsters broke into houses and forced defenceless women, children, and the elderly into their vehicles. When the vehicles were full of people, they were driven away to *Tuchinka* and unloaded into barracks.

For a whole day, the vehicles ran rounds through the ghetto. For a whole day, the drunken gang carried out their vile task. Around 18,000 Jews were extracted to *Tuchinka*. They were kept there for two days. The shouts and crying of children, exhausted by thirst, flung on top of one another like heaps of manure, filled the air all around. Then the machine guns began to stutter, and the lifeless, decapitated corpses of Soviet citizens cruelly murdered by Hitler's bloodthirsty dogs were flung into graves prepared for them in advance.

The pogrom only targeted some streets, rather than the whole ghetto: these were Respublikanskaya, Shevchenko, Nemiga, Khlebnaya and others.

By the evening of the 7th of November, the atrocities began to wind down. By the morning of the next day no vehicles were coming into the ghetto, but the Germans and the Polizei continued to throw their weight around, breaking windows and doors, climbing into homes, robbing, and forcing people outside, and then sending them to the *Judenrat*.

People were forced to crowd into the square from other streets with the aim of creating a district for "skilled workers". All of the labourers with their various areas of expertise were labelled "skilled workers" by the Germans and were resettled to a separate district. The result was another resettlement of Jews. There were Jews running around with packs on their shoulders trying to find refuge, the tears still drying around their eyes, fearing for their lives, their hearts aching with the loss of friends or relatives who had been killed.

In November 1941, 5000 Jews arrived in Minsk from Central Europe - the *Hamburg Jews*. They were settled in the spaces that had "become vacant" after the pogrom against the Belarusian Jews. Some streets (Nemiga and others) were reassigned to the *Russian District* by order of the Gestapo. The ghetto shrank in size. Those inside it went on living a hard, hungry life and even this was often snatched away early.

The 20th of November 1941. It was not yet morning, but the Germans and their Polizei were already walking the streets of the ghetto: Zamkovaya, Podzamkovaya, Zelyonaya, Sakharnaya and others. Once more, people were being forced out of their living quarters into columns and herded towards

Tuchinka to their graves. Partitions had been put up around the graves and people were thrown in still alive. There they were shot and burnt.

Another 8000 Jews were killed. In the ghetto the sound of crying and groaning was ceaseless. People would crawl into specially adapted cellars and disguised rooms which were given the name of *malinas* but even these didn't always save them. The German authorities' justification for the pogrom of the 20th of November was that the one on the 7th of November had "not been executed to plan": fewer Jews were killed than stipulated in the decree issued by the high command.

The formation of Desyatkas

The pogroms which were being carried out did not break the Jewish resistance; not even the deaths of its leaders stopped this movement. Weinhaus died in the pogrom of the 20th of November 1941. In his place Bruslin[29], the Propaganda[30] Secretary of the Voroshilovskiy District Party Committee in Minsk, was brought into the Party group. At the end of November, the communists managed to hold a shared Party conference whose leader was 'Slavek'. Gebelev was chosen to be Chairman of the Party group from the ghetto. From this time onwards, people began to be systematically sent to join the partisan detachments. The shared Party conference mandated that a Party organisation should be formed based on the principle of '*desyatkas*'. At the head of every *desyatka* was a secretary. *Desyatkas* were formed exclusively via personal connections and recommendations. Every secretary of a *desyatka* was linked to a higher figure of authority. The ghetto was one of the designated zones. The Party conference had effectively created an Underground Party Committee. 'Slavek' was chosen as its secretary.

Within the Minsk Party Committee Smolar was put in charge of the ghetto. He was the secretary of the Party group in the ghetto and was residing in the ghetto under the surname of Stolyarevich. He went by the Party nickname of "Modest". The heating plant at the Jewish hospital served as a headquarters where Smolar operated. Here the communists would gather and here, the most important and serious issues were discussed and resolved.

---

[29] Original name "Bruskind" but was changed to appear less Jewish.

[30] It is worth noting that in Russian, the word *propaganda* does not carry the same highly negative connotations as it does in English: the effect is closer to something like "ideology". (*Translator*)

The heads of the *desyatkas* were: Naum Feldman, Zyama Okun, Nadya Kuzir, Maizels, Rolbin, Rubenchik and others. Emma Rodova was appointed as signaller for contact with the communists of the Russian District. The following tasks were assigned to the *desyatkas*.

1. Nominate candidates from among the communists and combat-ready individuals to be sent off to the partisan detachments.
2. Gather weaponry.
3. Send material support to the partisan detachments in the form of warm clothes.
4. Gather and send medical supplies to the partisan detachments.
5. Create a fund to help the needy.

Winter was hard for inhabitants of the ghetto. They suffered from hunger, cold and the damp in their unheated living quarters. Jews working in the Russian District who had the chance to socialise with the Russian population were not so hard hit, but those Jews who did not work beyond the wire fence were hard up and went hungry. It was mainly the communists who did not go out to work that went hungry[31]. It was for these communists that the material support fund was created.

Thanks to links with Soviet citizens in the *Judenrat,* people were successfully placed to use their occupations on German work sites to the maximum advantage for themselves and for the struggle against the German occupiers. Groups of younger workers were placed on work sites linked with the production of weaponry and ammunition in order to give them the chance to steal from their workplace.

Women worked wherever there was a chance to get linen and warm clothes, and in this way, they were able to redirect such items to the partisan detachments. Regular packages were produced to be sent off to these detachments, most often in Ohnenheim's living quarters on 46 Respublikanskaya Street. Market places were used as the sites of gatherings. As a result of the detachments changing location, in February 1942 contact with some of the partisan detachments was lost and a search to find a detachment then began. There was intelligence that the Nechipurovich detachment was operating in the direction of Dukora. A group of people was gathered including Margolin the

---

[31] Many communists were in the underground resistance, and therefore could not risk going to Nazi-run worksites.

doctor, Skoblo – one of the first Stakhanovites[32] in the BSSR – and others. All of these went off to search for the detachment. The group were armed with four rifles, two revolvers and four grenades.

The expedition was unsuccessful. Its members were trapped and surrounded by the Gestapo. Many of them were killed, including Skoblo. Others returned to the ghetto having lost some of their extremities to frostbite and spent a long time in hospital. While some people began to search for detachments, others were looking for weaponry to buy and stockpile. Nauman [sic] Feldman was an expert at doing the latter.

On the instructions of the Party Committee, people looked for ways to organise escape for inhabitants of the ghetto who were unable to join the partisan detachments. In the early days when Soviet citizens had not yet experienced the worst of their persecution at the hands of the brutal fascists, they believed that it was enough to get people onto the other side of the wire fence and hand them over to the Russian District, hoping there would be a life guaranteed for them there. This was an attempt to snatch the most valuable kind of capital – human – from out of the hands of the executioner.

In February 1942 contact was established with the Soviet elements of the Minsk Administrative Board, under whose mediation the transfer of children out of the ghetto into Russian orphanages was being carried out. It remained only to do the same for women and the elderly.

The Party Underground Committee was looking for a way to send these children. Nina Liss was appointed for this purpose. She went to western Belarus to look for villages and farmsteads situated far away from railways and main roads where the children could go. People were looking for opportunities to free themselves from the heavy chains of slavery under Hitler and break out of the wire fence. They wanted to fight and die in battle, to avenge themselves for the wounds inflicted on them and the suffering caused to them. While the Jews were still reeling from one blow, another one was already being lined up for them.

In February 1942 Mushkin, Chairman of the *Judenrat*, was arrested. His role was a hard one: on the one hand, he was waging war against the occupiers by giving material support to the partisan detachments, but on the other hand he was obliged to uphold the pretence of maintaining normal relations with the German authorities and carrying out their directives and orders. He had to keep

---

[32] 'Stakhanovites' were workers who were heroised by the Soviet Union for their hyper-productivity. They were named after Aleksey Stakhanov, a Russian miner who allegedly mined 227 tonnes of coal in a single shift, breaking previous records.

his work secret from those members of the *Judenrat* who had sold out to the Germans, by whom he was surrounded: these were the likes of Rosenblat, Epstein, Markman, Kagan and Ginzburg. Mushkin's cover was blown by an informer. Mushkin was tortured and tormented for a long time in jail, but he suffered in silence and didn't give his comrades away. It was only a month after his arrest and torture that Mushkin was taken out of jail; he was killed while attempting to escape from a vehicle.

Winter of 1942

Then came the winter of 1942. It brought with it hunger, cold and disease. The pitiful existence that people endured would be hard to call "life". The crying of children and groans of the sick, left alone and uncared for, filled Jewish homes. People survived on scraps thrown out from German kitchens. Potato shavings became a widespread dish amongst the Jewish population; housewives worked out how to bake fritters and puddings out of them. Diseases spread: furunculosis, scurvy, typhus, and typhoid fever. These diseases had to be hidden from the German authorities, who required daily reports on numbers admitted to and discharged from hospitals. The Germans were afraid of infectious diseases spreading, so the Jews knew that as soon as the German authorities found out these kinds of diseases had appeared in the ghetto, a pogrom was inevitable. Even so, the fact that the German monsters were unaware of instances of disease in the ghetto, this did not stop pogroms raining down on the Jews with more horrific force than ever before.

On the morning of 2nd March 1942 passenger vehicles carrying Gestapo agents began to approach the ghetto. Among them was Obersturmführer Schmidt. He was already completely drunk. This did not bode well. The Jews began to be agitated. However, the work columns set off to work as normal, and the newly arrived 'guests' made themselves comfortable in the living quarters of Epstein, the head of the 'labour market', where they set about making merry. There was no shortage of food and expensive wines to be had. Provisions had been brought to the ghetto on a carrier vehicle. There were too many bloodthirsty dogs in the same place, all itching for Soviet blood; the space became too cramped for them, so they spilled out onto the street and the square too. A member of the Polizei was summoned to join the Gestapo agents: Richter, master of the 5th sector. He was an old police dog, who, in his own words, had "served in the police all his life"; the ghetto was under his jurisdiction.

The rowdy pack of fascists got drunk and stuffed their faces in the middle of the street, and then the executioners' 'work' began. They broke into houses with whips, revolvers and machine guns and forced everyone out into the yard by the shoe factory on Shpalernaya Street. Crowds of people – women, children, and the elderly – stood and waited to die. There were two houses on Tekhnicheskaya Street where the executioners couldn't find anyone because they were hiding in *malinas*. Therefore, the monsters set fire to the house from all sides and burned those people alive. In the morning scorched corpses were found amongst the ash. By five in the morning the work columns began to return from town. They were met at the gates of the ghetto by Gestapo agents. Together with the crowd of people waiting to die in the yard by the shoe factory they were sent to the railway, loaded into carriages, and taken in the direction of the city of Dzerzhinsk. There they were shot. Another 5000 Jews were killed. Many people tried to flee, but the bandits' bullets found their mark.

The Gestapo surrounded the column of jail workers, who were led by their foreman Levin, formerly an artist and children's writer who wrote under the pseudonym of Ber Sarin. He demanded that the whole column should be set free, making the point that his column was entirely composed of skilled workers. The Gestapo freed only him, but Levin insisted that everyone should be freed. He was beaten with rifle butts and chased away. Levin was holding a tin vessel in his hands and used it to attack the Germans. He was immediately shot in the middle of the street.

In the evening, as the bloody work was drawing to a close, Obersturmführer Schmidt, surrounded by his pack of wolves and some policemen all by now completely drunk, stood holding a long whip, lashing the air, wheeling round on his feet to face now left, now right, and shouted in perfect Russian: "Today has been such a success! A success! A fantastic success!" Polizeimeister Richter received an award and was promoted for organising the pogrom and supporting the Gestapo so well. Later he recounted to Epstein that the 'work' had begun late: at midday instead of early in the morning, and therefore, so as not to have to go rounding up people late at night, he had the workmen's columns taken instead, which, in his words, yielded "brilliant results". As with the first pogroms, those who were in the sanatorium and orphanage were killed, and some of the members of the *Judenrat* were killed.

A horrific scene ensued: a column of children of all ages, from toddlers to 13–14-year-olds, led by the head of the orphanage. The children were shouting: "What have we done to deserve this? Our soldiers are going to come and avenge our blood and the deaths of our mothers and fathers." Whiplashes came whistling down on the children's heads and the children, with swollen bloody marks and their faces puffy from being beaten, tattered and hungry, continued on their way. Whenever a child fell behind and couldn't keep up with the rest, he or she was shot dead on the spot. The whole road was strewn with the little corpses of children. Those left alive clenched their fists and their eyes burned with anger and hatred. "How long until the day of reckoning?" they asked each other. One of the carers, who was from Western Europe and who they called 'Amsterdam', not wishing to give herself up to the enemy alive, committed suicide by opening a vein.

The population of the ghetto decreased. There was another resettlement, where Jews were transferred from one living space to another, from one district to the next. Some of the streets were reassigned to the Russian District. The ghetto shrank in size and the cordon around it tightened.

The lull did not last long. The pogroms organised by the Gestapo didn't stop the work being carried out by the communists in the ghetto and the people escaping to join the partisan detachments, whose number grew larger every day. The Gestapo knew about this, and every instance of Jews escaping from the ghetto was punished with bloody acts of terror. In the language of the bandits, the reprisals taking place in the ghetto were called "exterminating the Bolshevist infection". In cases where the Gestapo found a trail leading to somebody linked to the Underground Party organisation, or who was considering escaping from the ghetto, they would hold responsible not only that person but all the inhabitants of the block where he or she lived, or the whole column of people with whom he or she worked. They would surround the block on all sides at night, take everybody out and shoot them.

Nighttime pogroms

At the end of March 1942, a wave of nighttime pogroms began. The inhabitants of the ghetto listened with horror to the stutter of machine guns in the night and the crying and shouts of the people being executed. At night one could hear the footfall of people running from bullets: some managed to save themselves, for the time being, others took a bullet in the back.

Nighttime pogroms took place on the 31st of March and the 3rd, 15th and 23rd of April. During the pogrom on the 31st of March 1942 Nina Liss was killed. She had just returned from Western Belarus where she had been carrying out a mission for the Party: finding places where people could be smuggled to once they were out of the ghetto.

It began when a traitor handed over lists of members of the Underground Party Committee to the Gestapo, which were so detailed they even gave the addresses in the ghetto where they were located.

Nina Liss lived at number 18 Kollektornaya Street. When the bandits surrounded the block that night they began to knock and shout: "Open up, Nina". The Gestapo agents demanded the handing over of Gebelev, Smolar, Feldman and Okun. They warned that if they refused to give these people up, all the members of the *Judenrat* would be shot. Ioffe, the newly appointed Chairman of the *Judenrat*, knew that the Germans would need very little provocation to carry out this threat, but equally, he couldn't carry out the Gestapo's order.

Gebelev had three surnames which he would use for different situations, so in the end the command of the Gestapo lost the trail and didn't know where to look for him. There were many Feldmans in the ghetto, so the Gestapo arrested three of them and sent them to jail, from where they never returned. As for Okun, it was not long before he was arrested.

Smolar (Stolyarevich), who headed the Underground Party organisation of the ghetto, was uncatchable. The Gestapo persistently demanded for him to be given up. Ioffe had a trick up his sleeve: he took a clean blank passport and filled it out with the details of 'Yefim Stolyarevich', then smeared it with blood and took it to the Gestapo, announcing that "this passport was found in one of the blocks where a nighttime pogrom had been carried out, and was removed from the clothes of one of the corpses." The Gestapo were satisfied, believing that Stolyarevich (Smolar) had been killed along with all the inhabitants of the block. Stolyarevich, Gebelev and Feldman lived on to continue the struggle with the enemy.

At this time, Feldman was taking care of the business of sourcing weaponry. The groups of people who were sent to join the partisan detachments armed themselves with rifles, revolvers, and grenades. Besides armaments, all the resistance's efforts were directed towards finding a printing press to intercept and send out to the detachments. Two presses were intercepted and sent and a third was left to the disposal of the Municipal Party Committee.

The Gestapo justified their nighttime pogroms as part of the fight against the partisan movement, even as they strove to rout the Party's forces. Similar actions were also carried out in the Russian District. An enemy infiltrator managed to find his way into the Party organisation resulting in the arrest of some of the members of the Underground Party Committee.

Gebelev transported ten people who were communists from the Russian District into the ghetto under Jewish passports and hid them in *malinas*. On the day of the pogrom carried out against the Party leadership in the Russian District, 40 people were sent out of the ghetto to join the partisans. Five kilometres from the city, the detachment's command was supposed to meet the newcomers. However, the arrests of members of the Party leadership, in the Russian District and the ghetto, resulted in this meeting not taking place. Some of the newcomers died on their way, while the rest returned to the ghetto.

The nighttime pogrom of the 23rd of April 1942 was especially harsh. Blocks on Obuvnaya, Sukhaya, Shornaya and Kollektornaya were surrounded. The pogrom began at 5pm and was only finished by 11pm. Around 500 people were killed.

Another stunningly harsh nighttime pogrom happened in July 1942. On Zavalnaya Street two densely populated four storey blocks were surrounded. They were set on fire from all sides and their inhabitants burned alive. Several hundred people were killed.

Every day and night brought with it new victims. The German thugs changed: some of the old ones left and other new ones arrived. They lorded it over the ghetto. The task of exterminating the Jews continued to be carried out by the leadership of each one of these groups under the pretence of keeping order.

Not long before he left the ghetto, Richter decided to test whether the order issued by the German authorities of 'mandatory attendance at work for all' was being implemented in practice. He went outside, stopped the first three Jews he came across, took them to the labour office and ordered the policemen who were accompanying him to undress the Jews. He beat them half to death, took one outside into the square and tied him to a post, forced everyone to come outside and shot him dead in front of them all. A piece of cardboard was hung on the chest of the dead man with the following notice: "Anyone who dares not go to work will be dealt with in this way".

A new Polizeimeister, Göttenbach, replaced Richter. He issued an order for the ghetto to be turned into a camp. All the blocks in the ghetto were given numbers and besides the yellow patch, its inhabitants had to wear the number of the block they lived in sewn onto their clothes. Göttenbach personally shot hundreds of Jews for disobeying this order. Not that any reason needed to be given for shooting Jews. During the month of May three Jewish labourers were brought to the ghetto from Trostenets[33]. Feeling ill, they attempted to be seen by a doctor, but instead Göttenbach took them to the cemetery and shot them. There were many similar incidents.

The Jews bided their time. Working at the 'October' factory was considered the most profitable occupation. Besides 200 grams of bread, prisoners were given a mug of hot water which they called "coffee", and there was watery soup for lunch.

---

[33] A death camp.

In May 1942 thirteen women were sacked. They were not allowed to talk to their boss about the reason for their sacking, but they decided to go with the column to the factory to find out what they had been sacked for. They were given permission to speak to their boss, and then the thirteen hungry, swollen Jewish women were put in jail. They were tormented and worn down for two long, hard weeks in jail, and then brought to the ghetto in a reinforced convoy and lined up in the square opposite the *Judenrat*. Everybody was forced to come outside and there, in full view, the thirteen Jewish women were shot dead with explosive bullets. Their corpses lay where they were in the square for two days; it was forbidden to clear them away.

In April 1942 an order was issued by the Gestapo obliging all Jews to come to the square where the *Judenrat* was held every Sunday at 10am sharp. Even on Sundays the police and the Germans gave the Jews no peace, forcing them all outside to come to the square. There were always beatings with whips and rifle butts. The Jews would be in a state of tense anticipation, not knowing what would be waiting for them in the square. Every Sunday at this assembly, which the Germans called an 'appell', Richter, Göttenbach, Fichtel, Menschel and other such dogs read speeches urging the Jews not to leave the ghetto to join the partisan detachments, insisting that the ghetto was the safest place for the Jews and that there would be no more pogroms. Every Sunday they would gather the Jews together in the square and repeat these same speeches, after which they would make them perform concert pieces, sing, and play instruments, and often take photographs.

One such Sunday the Polizei went to check each house to make sure that the Jews had gone to the Appell, and in one house they found eleven men. They brought them to the square, showed them to everybody and explained that they were going to take them to jail, never to return again. And so, they did. The eleven people were shot in jail. The appells continued until the 10th of June 1942.

Wherever the fascists and their underlings went, Jews lost the right to even exist. One Sunday after an appell a group of Jews were standing by a water pipe on Tankovaya Street. Some policemen were passing down 2nd Opanskiy Lane with a woman. They went up to the wire and saw the people queueing for water. The policeman turned to the woman and said: "Look what a good shot I am". Then he fired a shot into the crowd with his rifle. The Jews scattered. The street was now empty save the body of 10-year-old Esther Grunfest lying by the water pipe in a pool of blood. Some people ran up and carried Esther away. An hour later she died. Incidents like this were not unusual.

One group of Germans and policemen went into Jewish living quarters on Tankovaya Street with the aim of robbing it. A man called Volodya Paleyev stood waiting outside in the yard. He did not go into the block. Even this angered the bandits. A shot rang out from the window which found its mark and killed Paleyev.

Due to the arrest of Party Committee members, the guides from the partisan detachments stopped coming to Minsk. Contact was temporarily lost. The Party Committee of the ghetto discussed the situation at hand and came to the conclusion that it was necessary to get people out to the detachments. Groups were chosen to leave, 20 at a time and the first group was headed by Lapidus. The transfer was to take place in a vehicle, but since not all the people included in the transfer would fit into one vehicle it was agreed that the vehicle should take the first group of 20 people to a distance of 45 kilometres outside the city, and then the same vehicle would come back to within 15 kilometres in the direction of the city, where the second group would meet it on foot, and the vehicle would take them to the same place as the first.

The second group of people set off on foot at the agreed time. Among them were Feldman, Tumin, Livshits and others. But when they reached the agreed place, the vehicle was nowhere to be found, nor the guide. The first party of people made it to safety, but the second came under fire from Ukrainian traitors. Some of these – Feldman and Tumin – managed to return to the ghetto. Some were killed on the way. For some time, the search for the detachments came to nothing. It was difficult establishing contact not only with the partisan detachments but even with the communists from the Russian District. The whole period of April 1942 was spent trying to make contact.

In late April 1942 the remaining communists in the ghetto were trying to establish contact and consider re-establishing the Municipal Party organisation. To this end a Party meeting was convened at which a group of communists from the Russian District appeared and announced that it was they who were the leaders of the Underground Party organisation in Minsk. Following that meeting a Party organisation was re-established not based on the principle of *desyatkas* as before but on the territorial-industrial principle. The Party organisation of the ghetto was assigned to the Kaganovich District Committee of the Party as an independent organisational unit.

With the help of the Underground Party Committee, an expedition in the direction of Slutsk was mustered under the command of Captain Nikitin. The Jews of the ghetto were sent south of Minsk with this detachment. Some of Lapidus's men also joined. Prisoners of war working in the camp on Shirokaya Street, the felt factory and other work sites, were systematically smuggled out.

Whilst smuggling prisoners of war out to the detachments over the wire fence, Gebelev was arrested. He was a fearless and tireless patriot who gave his life for his homeland, sacrificing it for the struggle with the enemy. As prisoners of war were being smuggled out to the detachments, sabotage missions were being carried out on work sites, the meat processing plant, the factory, and the distillery. A Jewish blacksmith was systematically smuggling out spirits that were meant to reach the war front.

The party committee sent Naum Feldman, one of the members of the Underground Party organisation of the ghetto, to organise a detachment base to the west. Feldman had a hard journey lasting two days and nights. He was expecting to meet with a guide nine kilometres outside the city who would take him and his group to the appointed place. A detachment newly formed under Skachkov found the group, but Skachkov refused to take Feldman's group in. Feldman therefore decided to put together his own detachment, but for this he would need to acquire weaponry and strengthen the cohesion of his group. There was no commanding body. Feldman sent messengers to the Underground Committee of the ghetto, who sent him new comrades. The group armed themselves with handheld machine guns, rifles, revolvers, and pistols. At the end of May 1942 Nikitin, in Slutsk, took some of these people and weaponry to become part of his detachment. Those left busied themselves searching for weaponry. There was still no commanding body. Again, the Underground Committee of the ghetto came to the rescue. A commanding body was sent. A while later this had to be replaced. Contact with the Party Committee of the ghetto remained constant. In June 1942 a new brigade commander was sent to lead a detachment, Semyon Grigoryevich Ganzenko, a prisoner of war from the camp on Shirokaya Street, for whom an escape had previously been orchestrated. The detachment was named for Budyonny[34]. Feldman worked in this detachment as a Party organiser. The detachment was added to the Stalin brigade and became one of the battle detachments. Later, Ganzenko would be appointed Commander and Feldman Commissar of one of the detachments of the brigade.

July 1942 pogroms

All of these escapes from the ghetto were fraught with colossal difficulties. The ghetto was guarded day and night. Ambushes were set at every turn. The Gestapo managed to organise some of the Jewish Militia to do their bidding: Markin, Kagal, Ginzburg and Rosenblat with Epstein at their head. These people reported everything that happened in the ghetto to the Gestapo. They

---

[34] Semyon Mikhaylovich Budyonny was one of the first Marshals of the Soviet Union, the highest rank in the Red Army.

were loyal helpers of the Gestapo. Some of the leaders and active members of the underground organisation fell into the hands of the Gestapo as a result of their reports.

On the 27th of June 1942 the Gestapo issued an order that from the 28th of July 1942, besides the yellow patches and block numbers, every Jew would now have to wear another distinguishing badge: red for workers and green for the dependents of workers and the unemployed. Workers would receive their badges from their places of work and everyone else would receive theirs in the square at the *Judenrat*. The order informed its readers that since the *Judenrat* would take a while to get all the badges handed out on their own, on the 28th of July the Gestapo would be handing out badges themselves.

On the morning of the day indicated, after the work columns had departed, some Gestapo agents and policemen arrived in the ghetto headed by Gattenbach. The whole ghetto was surrounded with a tight cordon of patrols. Inhabitants were forced out of their living quarters onto the square. Large, covered vehicles carrying mobile gas chambers began to drive towards the ghetto. People were loaded into them. Inside, they were gassed, and their dead bodies driven off to pre-dug graves. Those people who were at the sanatorium and the children in the orphanage were killed.

During earlier pogroms the hospital had not been touched, but this time it was destroyed. A feral band of men broke into the hospital. Patients were shot where they lay in their beds. One of those to be killed was Kroshner, a decorated veteran. Medical personnel and doctors in their white gowns were lined up in a separate column and taken to the square. There they were loaded into *dushegubkas* and exterminated. 48 doctors were killed, the greatest experts in the BSSR: Professor and Doctor of Medical Sciences, Senior Lecturer Maizels, Candidate of Medical Sciences, and other very senior and experienced doctors: Trugel, Kantorovich, Gurvich, Sirotkina and many others.

Individuals who showed the slightest sign of resistance were shot dead on the spot. The whole ghetto was bathed in blood and corpses lay all around. On Sukhaya Street all the Jews were taken out of their blocks and *malinas*. One of these people was thrown to the ground; sheets of glass were removed from some nearby windows and placed on top of him, then someone else was made to stamp on the glass so that it would cut him. Seeing that the Jew entrusted with this task was not doing a good job, the villains stamped the glass into pieces themselves and then tortured both of them to death.

The terrible, unprecedented pogrom carried on the 28th, 29th, 30th and 31st of July 1942 until 6 o'clock in the evening. During the short breaks which the executioners organised for themselves they drank and revelled. Tables covered with white cloth were placed right in the middle of the street. As the ghetto was bathed in blood, their drunken shouts and laughter filled the air. Hitler's thugs were washing down their vile, barbaric 'work' with barrels full of wine. During those bloody days the *Judenrat* was surrounded on all sides by guards.

On the evening of the 29th of July 1942 Chairman Ioffe, his deputy Blumenstock and the doctor, Larno, who was present at the time, were summoned. They were taken out onto Tankovaya Street and shot. The corpses lay where they were until the pogrom was over. On the night between the 29th and 30th of July 1942 the guards informed the *Judenrat* that tomorrow morning the question of whether to keep them alive or execute them would be resolved. Gattenbach confirmed that this was the case. On the 30th of July all members of the *Judenrat* and police were loaded into *dushegubkas* and sent away. Among those killed was Zorev, a decorated veteran and performer at the Belorussian Drama Theatre.

On the 31st of July 1942 at one o'clock the order was given to halt the pogrom. But nothing could stop the fascist barbarians from their revelry. Their thirst for blood was not yet satisfied and so like wild beasts they ran from house to house looking for *malinas*, dragging people out and shooting them. Only by the evening was the pogrom over. Gattenbach gathered the *Judenrat* policemen who were still alive and ordered them to clear away the corpses. When the working columns returned to the ghetto (on pogrom days they were kept back at their work sites in the Russian District), coagulated clots of blood from the people who had been shot could be seen in the streets. On their return the workers found that their friends and relatives were missing from their empty ransacked houses. The ghetto resounded with cries and sobbing.

The ghetto on the night of the 1st of August was a horrific scene: tear-stained eyes and the faces of mothers and fathers driven out of their minds with grief on returning to find their children missing from home, or present but dead. The corpses which were outside had been cleared, but those which had been inside buildings had not. The handful of Jews left in the city of Minsk wept and groaned. No family was without its victims. Out of 75,000 Jews, by the 1st of August 1942 just 8,724 were left alive.

German Jews (the *Hamburg Jews*) also fell victim to this pogrom. 3000 Jews from the German ghetto were sent away in *dushegubkas*. It was announced to the German Jews that they had to pack their bags. Supposedly, they were to be sent to work. Obersturmführer Gattenbach read a speech in front of the Jews in the square and then they were loaded into the vehicles and gassed.

Once again there was a resettlement and once again people were dragged from one place to another. A considerable portion of the area of the ghetto was reassigned to the Russian District. The cordon around the ghetto tightened. The German dogs in charge changed over and Richter left. He was replaced by Gattenbach, then Fichtel, then Mendel. Every arrival of a new German dog or departure of an old one, cost human lives. Those brutes grew rich on Jewish goods. After every pogrom the Jews who were taken away left belongings behind them and the fascists took these for themselves.

January 1943 - Liquidation of the Ghetto

In January 1943 the corpses of some Germans were found in the Russian District. The Gestapo punished this with terrible acts of repression. On the 1st of February 1943 at 3 o'clock in the afternoon covered vehicles carrying mobile gas chambers entered the ghetto. Out of them came Gestapo agents led by Obersturmführer Miller, a fascist with the blood of many German citizens on his hands. People were snatched in the middle of the street and loaded into the *dushegubkas*. Even labourers were forced outside and loaded into the vehicles. By morning there were 401 people missing from the ghetto.

Not long afterwards 53 Jews from the city of Slutsk arrived in Minsk. They had been brought in as "skilled workers". They told stories of the horrors of the gradual liquidation of the ghetto in their city and would often mention Ribbe, an agent of the Gestapo notable for his exceptional cruelty.

During the first half of February 1943 two German figures appeared on the scene in the ghetto. Their clothing bore the distinguishing marks of the Gestapo. One day while walking down the street they stopped a Jewish woman, searched her, found eight stamps, confiscated them, and carried on walking. Another Jewish woman with her four-year-old son crossed their path. They stopped her and asked (one of them, the translator Michelson, spoke Russian) why she was not working. The woman presented a sick note, but instead of discussing the matter they both attacked her, beat her up and dragged her and her child to the cemetery, where they shot them. On the way back from the cemetery they came across a boy of about 15 years old holding two chunks of firewood in his hands. They asked him: "Where did you get the wood?" He replied: "My boss gave it to me at work." They dragged him to the cemetery and shot him. That evening when the labourers returned from work the Slutsk Jews recognised their old executioner. "That's Ribbe with his translator Michelson," they said, "he must be here to start liquidating the ghetto".

They were right. These men turned out to be the infamous executioner, Gestapo Hauptscharführer[35] Ribbe - expert conductor of pogroms against the Jews (who had been rewarded several times for his actions during pogroms), and his helper and translator Michelson.

From the moment Ribbe arrived the Jews were not given a moment's peace. His trusty helpers in the bloody reprisal which he wreaked on the Jews were Michelson, the newly appointed Polizeimeister Bunge, and his deputy Feldwebel Scherner. From early morning until late at night these four rabid dogs patrolled the ghetto. For every step they took one Jew fell dead. If Ribbe took a dislike to somebody's face, they were shot. If Ribbe thought somebody's patch was not properly sewn on, they were shot.

The streets of the ghetto emptied. People were afraid to go outdoors, but it made no difference as Ribbe's pack of wolves searched for them in their homes instead. If they found a piece of German bread, Jews were shot. If they found a map or a book to read, you would be shot. For any crime, anywhere you were shot. Hundreds of people were shot by Ribbe, Michelson, Bunge, and Scherner who had lost all semblance of humanity.

Starving Jewish children would find their way into the Russian District to sit on the streets and beg for scraps of bread. They would normally gather by the railway bridge in the evening to wait for the work columns and return to the ghetto with them. In February 1943 a round-up was organised to catch these Jewish children. They were caught in the Russian District, loaded into a carrier vehicle, taken to the Jewish cemetery, and shot. Fifteen hungry, worn out little Jewish children met their deaths at the hands of the fascist executioner.

Ribbe had no qualms about hiring the most questionable people to work for him. The infamous thief, drunkard and pervert from Warsaw Yefim Rosenblat, a man who served fascism with his heart and soul, was made Chief of the Jewish Militia. Rosenblat had many bloody deeds on his conscience. Like a dog he spied on the Jews, listening to their every whisper and watching their every movement. Together with Ribbe he helped to undertake the "extermination of the Bolshevist infection". He handed over communists and people linked to the Underground Party organisation and the partisan movement.

Ribbe was not satisfied with Rosenblat and decided to take him out of the picture and replace him with another more capable spy. Rosenblat knew too much; he was one more undesirable witness. Ribbe made a remark to Rosenblat

---

[35] Hauptscharführer - Head squad leader

about the insufficient number of partisans he had caught. Rosenblat's reply to this, in the presence of members of the *Judenrat*, was: "Yes, mister Hauptführer! I will do better, but I have already contributed greatly to the struggle against the partisans and Mr. Gattenbach knows this. Ask him." But there was no help for him. In February Rosenblat was arrested by Ribbe in the middle of the street and sent to jail where he was shot. Rosenblat had sold himself to the fascists, and the fascists were his downfall.

The post of Chief of the Jewish Militia then fell to Naum Epstein, in addition to the post he already held as head of the Jewish labour market. Concerning this, Ribbe said: "The Gestapo trusts him more than anyone else." The Gestapo knew their man. They knew that Epstein had sold himself to the Germans a while back for a bottle of wine, for butter and lard, for a good life, for the chance to rob his brothers with total freedom. This rascal sold his own people wholesale. He made his militiamen spy on people and report even the tiniest misdemeanours to him. He in turn reported these to Miller and as a result of the reports some of the best people in the ghetto, committed to the Bolshevik Party's cause, disappeared.

February 1943 is famous as the month when pogroms began on the very first day. On the 19th of February 1943 Ribbe was driving on a tour of the sites where German Jews were working when his attention was caught by some young attractive women. He selected thirteen of these beauties: twelve German Jews and one Russian Jew – Lina Neu. The women were young, beautiful, and full of strength and energy. Their executioner ordered them to appear at the Labour Market in the ghetto for 10 o'clock. Epstein brought thirteen of the Jewish "operatives" (workers) to arrive at the same time. That sell-out dog knew what the women had been gathered for and was thirsty for blood.

Ribbe and Michelson arrived at the Labour Market. The victims were still unaware of their fate. Outside it was noisy. The work columns were coming home, and many people stopped and waited: everybody was curious as to why Ribbe had gathered the most beautiful women. The Jews were worried. Ribbe gave an order: each of the workers present was to take a woman by the arm and walk down Sukhaya Street at a steady pace. A groan ran through the ghetto: "Sukhaya Street – they're going to the cemetery to be shot."

It was a terrible sight: thirteen young couples walking in a stately procession down the street to the gates of the cemetery. One of the German Jews asked if she could say goodbye to her husband. Ribbe said that she could. He was taken to the cemetery and shot with his wife watching. The brutes made the women strip naked and made a mockery of them, then Ribbe and Michelson did the work of the firing squad themselves. Such was the bandit's lack of human feeling that he took off Lina Neu's bra and put it in his pocket. "To remind me of a beautiful Jewish girl", he said to Epstein, who was present.

Epstein was proud of the trust which he was shown. The Gestapo had made the right choice with him. That evening the brute sold out another 140 people. That same terrible evening of the 19th of February 1943 Epstein did not go to bed. He was waiting for "news". At eleven o'clock in the evening a carrier vehicle entered the ghetto with Gestapo agents inside. Stopping on their way to pick up Epstein, they set off in the direction of Block no. 48 on Obuvnaya Street. Before people could put their heads out of their windows to see what was going on, the block was surrounded on all sides. People were taken out into the street and stood in single file; the crying of children was drowned out by machine-gun fire. 140 people were killed. Epstein calmly surveyed the pile of corpses. It fell to the local Jewish workers to drag the corpses away to the cemetery. Pools of blood remained visible on Obuvnaya Street for a long time after.

That terrible night two women, a man and a small boy managed to survive. The block was sealed up. Peoples' belongings were driven off to Ribbe and Epstein's lodgings. On the 20th of February 1943 Ribbe suggested hanging out an announcement informing the inhabitants of the ghetto that block no. 48 had been storing weaponry and it was for this crime that all those in the block had been shot. Everyone was to hand their weapons in to Epstein. If anyone did not want to bring them in person, they could drop them off anonymously. The order included a warning that if anybody was to refuse to hand over their weapons more mass killings such as this would follow. The Jews read this order with disgust, but the German fascists never got their weaponry, even though it was coming into the ghetto every day and being redirected to the partisan detachments.

The two women who had managed to survive came to their boss with a request to be given at least some of their own belongings which had been left in the building. Their boss brought an appeal to Ribbe who suggested that the women come and see him, and when they came, he arrested them and put them in a bunker specially adapted for arrests at the Labour Market. The women stayed in this shed for two days before Ribbe sent Michelson to get them. Michelson started calling out to them to come to the cemetery with him. Realising what was in store for them, the women flatly refused to follow him. He shot them on the spot, in the shed, in full sight of everybody present.

Ribbe liquidated the ghetto slowly, with no sense of hurry. He informed everybody that there would be no more pogroms, that he had been sent to the ghetto to keep the peace among the Jews and restore order. He brought the work columns under his own control: every evening together with Michelson he would meet the labourers and check their packs. He took away everything the labourers owned right down to potatoes and flour. If he ever found a bottle of milk or fat on a labourer, he would immediately confiscate these products: Jews often paid for this food with their lives. "Offenders" were driven away to the cemetery to be shot, and the foodstuffs were taken to Ribbe and Michelson's lodgings.

Ribbe asserted that he was chasing down Jews who were undertaking political activity and were involved in the partisan movement. Any time Ribbe realised that a person had disappeared from a work column, he would shoot the whole column. In this way the working columns of the distillery, the jail, the printing house, and many others were destroyed. The Jews working in the jail were warned that they did not have the right to talk about the horrors of the fascist jail in public. They were obliged to keep all of the barbaric acts which they had witnessed a secret. In order to isolate them and prevent them from speaking, even to the Jews from the ghetto, they were housed in barracks on the grounds of the jail.

In May 1943 on the orders of Ginter, who was in charge of the jail, all the Jewish labourers working in the jail were lined up, stripped naked, loaded into a vehicle, taken out of town, and shot. "They knew too much," said Ginter. After this Ginter came to Epstein requesting to be given new labourers. Epstein didn't tell the Jews the truth about where he was sending them, instead saying that he was assigning them "good work". He gathered a group of people and took them to the jail. Three weeks later they too were shot.

In the process of killing Jews, Ribbe came to the conclusion that children and the elderly had to be finished off. An order was issued to the Jewish Militia to bring all children who had no parents to the Labour Market. The little children were brought, all hungry in their tattered clothing. Some of those children did in fact have parents. This was the work of Kira Markman, Ilya Ginzburg and Kagan Samuil. The children were taken off to jail in a vehicle and then to the firing squad.

Scherner and Bunge tried to outdo their boss. One day Scherner was walking towards the work columns and saw that a mother was taking her child to work with her. After the recent killings of children, mothers were afraid to leave their children at home and so dragged them along to work, often carrying them in sacks. Scherner walked up to the vehicle, dragged the six-year-old child out, threw him onto the road, stepped on the child's neck with his boot, crushed it, trampled the child with his boots and threw the dead, disfigured child to one side. Having committed this terrible evil deed, he went and reported it to Bunge. Bunge, not wanting to lose face in front of his deputy, went to the work columns on the next day, seized a 17-year-old lad, took him to the cemetery and shot him. He then returned to the column, took another lad, and led him off towards the cemetery, shooting him on Sukhaya Street. That was how 20th century Hitlerian culture dealt with children.

The elderly and unemployed were also considered undesirables by the German fascists. "Elderly" could be used as a term for Jews of any age (25, 30, 40 years) to whom Michelson, Scherner, Bunge or even Epstein took a dislike. "Unemployed" referred to people who did not turn up to work for whatever reason, even those who had a note exempting them for two or three days.

The ghetto was shrinking noticeably, and the number of its inhabitants reduced daily. The prediction of the Slutsk Jews, that Ribbe had been sent to Minsk to liquidise the ghetto, proved correct. As a matter of policy Ribbe endeavoured to make sure that the truth about his despicable actions stayed within the bounds of the ghetto, but without success. Despite his best efforts, the truth about the vile actions he was committing became known even to German officers. There was a German officer – Inspector Schultz – working in the Luftwaffe. He made an agreement with the Jews who were working for him that he would get them out of the ghetto. He put 37 people into a carrier vehicle, armed them with machine guns, revolvers, and rifles, stole a radio transmitter to take with them and set off together with the Jews to join one of the partisan detachments.

Targeting the doctors and hospitals

The rampage of Hitler's vermin continued. Now that many of the children, the "unemployed" and the "elderly" had been dealt with, it was the turn of the doctors. At the end of April 1943 Ribbe gave an order to compile a list of doctors. The order was carried out. A few days later a new command came - all doctors were obliged to appear at the *Judenrat*. Nobody but Epstein knew what the doctors were needed for.

Once they had gathered, the doctors were lined up in a column. Epstein announced that he was taking them to the German Jewish ghetto, but actually took them to the Gestapo. Ribbe received them in a separate office. The conversation did not last long. They realised what Ribbe wanted to say and why he had gathered them there. Ribbe pointed out to Epstein that some of the doctors were elderly, such as Doctor Pechmann, and some were disabled, such as doctor Kantsevaya who had a limp. He asked Epstein to treat them with care, and to be careful when taking them across the city so that nobody got tired or lagged behind. Everybody was amazed that a monster like Ribbe should take such care. They were amazed, but also alarmed. He always acted kindly preceding pogroms.

Ribbe warned all the doctors that they had to appear at the Jewish Labour Market at 4 o'clock that same day. The doctors arrived. Ribbe and Michelson were already waiting for them. They quickly split the doctors up into groups - the geriatricians Shmotkin and Kantsevaya; paediatricians, Savvina and Lev; doctors from the Sanatorium and the Orphanage. Most of the internal organ specialists, otolaryngologists and stomatologists were put in a separate group. Ribbe's guard dog, Michelson, stood at the doorway guarding the exit and let nobody in.

The doctors selected were taken to a bunker and as soon as it got dark, their families were sent for. Lev's husband, Ilinskiy, a historian who had worked at a research institute was brought with their two children, Doctor Shmotkina's son, Doctor Savchik's three children and many others. By 5 o'clock in the morning over 100 people had been gathered. Before the work columns had left, Bunge and Scherner arrived with a Polizei detachment and took the column to jail. There, people's clothes were torn off and they were beaten, then shot. Yet another batch of doctors with their families was destroyed. While she was being taken to jail, the twelve-year-old daughter of Doctor Savchik shouted out: "Don't worry mummy, be brave, our blood will be avenged!"

The sanatorium and the orphanage were next on the list. One bright moonlit night at the end of April 1943 at 11 o' clock, two vehicles approached the large two-storey building where children, the disabled and the staff supporting them were housed. One was a passenger vehicle and the other a carrier vehicle. Ribbe and Michelson got out of the passenger vehicle and approached the building to point it out. Then they got back into the vehicle and drove away. The building was on Zaslavskaya Street right on the border with the Russian District. A whole pack of fascists ran out of the carrier vehicle, cut through the wire fence, and surrounded the house. Children and staff were snatched unclothed from their beds and thrown into the vehicle. The disabled, patients and younger children were shot where they were. In an hour the "work" was over. The carrier vehicle and its load of people drove away to the jail. Nobody ever saw these people again: they were killed, just as had happened to dozens of other people like them. The rooms inside the block were covered in endless pools of blood: spilled entrails and clots of blood filled the building. Bunge and Scherner came to do an inspection. They looked at their own handiwork with admiration and discovering several heavily wounded women, finished them off on the spot.

Next to the large official building stood a little shack which housed the orphanage's isolation unit. There were 30 sick children inside. All of the sick children were shot and when the bullets ran out Scherner and Bunge battered the remaining children to death with their fists. Epstein sent his militiamen to clear the corpses away.

Testimonies of Tragedy and Resistance in the Minsk Ghetto

The hospital was next in line. Ribbe arrived there in May 1943. He showed an interest in the state of the patients and asked to be shown the wards. Two days later in bright, warm weather at precisely 12 o'clock the ghetto's inhabitants heard gunshots coming from the hospital in the German Jewish ghetto. They raced over there. In the yard stood a large black *dushegubka*. The German Jews told them that Miller, Ribbe, Michelson and another four people dressed in civilian clothes with machine guns under their coats had turned up at the hospital and orphanage. There, they shot the patients and children. The bandits then went straight to the Russian Jews' hospital and surrounded it on all sides, but the patients started jumping out from the second floor. A few people managed to escape in this way. All the remaining patients were shot where they lay in their beds.

The hospital staff were ordered to clear away the corpses, clean the blood off everything and put the place in order so that the hospital would be back up and running and ready to receive new patients by 4 o'clock. Ribbe stressed that "the German authorities do not conduct pogroms: but they do need healthy people, not sick ones." The Russian Jewish ghetto was being destroyed and the German Jewish ghetto was nearing the end of its existence.

Targeting other workers

Those monsters prowled from house to house, looking into every nook and hunting people down. "What is your occupation? Where do you work? That job's too tough for you, we'll give you a new one. Let's send you to the camp to peel potatoes," Ribbe would say to the German Jews, adding: "You are to come to the Labour Market for 2 o'clock." Some naïve people thought that Ribbe really was going to offer them easy labour and asked for permission to bring members of their family with them. Ribbe allowed this "so as not to separate loved ones from each other".

Ribbe chose 175 of the German Jews. At 2 o'clock he went to Epstein's place, had lunch with him and drank wine and vodka, and then went into the yard and ordered all the Jewish militiamen to gather and be ready for "operations". Since he had some time to fill, he decided to have a bit of fun: he wanted a concert. Epstein obligingly suggested that Ostakh, the militiaman, play something on his violin. At that moment, Baratz, a violinist who had played in the Warsaw Philharmonic and then the Minsk Philharmonic orchestras, was passing by. He was walking past the German Jewish ghetto and could see the Jews gathering at Ribbe's order. He realised that another pogrom was about to happen. Suddenly Epstein stopped him, called him over and presented him to Ribbe. "Would you like him to play you something? This man is a very fine violinist. He can play you anything you like," suggested Epstein obligingly. Baratz protested in vain that he was in no fit state to play anything after his two-year break from the violin, but to no avail, he was forced to play. His face pale and with tears in his eyes, Baratz played to his executioners.

When the concert was over Ribbe let Baratz go, gathered the militiamen, and led them to the German Jewish ghetto. Within 10 minutes they had gathered a crowd of people with their children and locked them up in a bunker. A few minutes later a large, covered vehicle drove up. The people were loaded into it and the militiamen accompanied them to jail. They were driven out of the ghetto in total macabre silence. By this time the work columns were coming back into the ghetto. Seeing that a pogrom was in progress in the ghetto people began to get unsettled. They stopped by the ghetto gates, but the Polizei would not let them stay standing in the Russian District and forced them inside. Ribbe went up to the vehicles, made all the labourers get out and ordered the vehicles to drive up to the bunker and be loaded with the German Jews and driven away to jail. There the Jews were received by Richter and Menzel who undressed them, hosed them down with water from a pump, humiliated them in all kinds of ways and then shot them. Another 173 people were killed. The Jews were breaking their backs doing slave labour and were always looking for ways out so that they could throw off their hated chains. Many were killed in their search for a way to escape.

There were 44 Jews working at "Forflegunsamt[36]": Shoemakers, tailors, smiths, and painters. A communist named Yura Reutskiy and his friend Ilya Dukorskiy were working there among them. Reutskiy would often say to his comrades at work that he would go down fighting, that any Hitlerite who raised a hand against him would not live to tell the tale. In preparation for this he made himself a Finnish knife[37] which he would always carry with him. The work was on Dolgobrodskaya Street and to eat lunch (i.e., drink the meagre soup) they would go behind a bakery which stood several blocks away.

One day during the lunch break, Reutskiy met an old acquaintance called Savich, the former manager of the canteen at Belgosstroy[38]. Savich introduced himself as a patriot of the Soviet homeland, explaining that he was connected to the partisan detachments and their guides. He was on a mission to obtain a large amount of weaponry and could pay money. Two days later

---

[36] Possible German factory – unverifiable.

[37] Finnish knives (Finnish: puukko) were famous and became very popular in the Russian Empire and Soviet Union. The term came to be used for any knife with a straight blade and bevelled handle, whether Finnish or otherwise.

[38] **Belgosstroy** - short for *Belorusskoye gosudarstvennoye stroitelnoe* (Belarusian State Construction).

Reutskiy agreed to meet with Savich in order to give him a final answer about the number of weapons he could obtain. Reutskiy thought about Savich's proposition and decided to test him since he had a bad feeling about him, but the traitor Savich got there first. Savich turned up at "Forflegunsamt" with his boss Kovalyov and a band of Gestapo agents. Kovalyov quickly proceeded to the workshop. Savich stood watching him. The rest of the bandits surrounded the building. Kovalyov got to work searching the place. Reutskiy realised why the Gestapo were visiting their workshops. He and Dukorskiy glanced at each other. Dukorskiy slammed the door shut and Reutskiy, grabbing his knife, began stabbing Kovalyov. Kovalyov was bleeding everywhere but he stood his ground. The Gestapo men came running. Reutskiy and Dukorskiy were shot where they stood as the Gestapo attempted to arrest everyone else.

The labourers Mekhovskiy and Silberstein shouted to their comrades: "Don't let them take you alive! Run! Don't cry, don't ask for mercy!" Everybody ran, jumping over fences and hedges. Nobody was taken alive. Misha Belostokskiy made it across two fences before they caught up and riddled him with 20 bullets. Amongst the labourers was the sixteen-year-old son of the Blacher family. He too ran, but one of the bullets caught up with him. The Germans awarded Kovalyov the Order of the Iron Cross[39] for his struggle against the partisans.

Another bloody act of treachery took place on the 8th of May 1943. The head of the Housing Department of the *Judenrat* Solomon Blumin always helped the partisan movement in whatever way he could. After the Party[40] Organisation had been rumbled, guides coming to the ghetto from the detachments had to just hope that they were met by the right people. Blumin had trouble getting in contact with a guide to help him break out of the ghetto. With the help of an acquaintance called Sonka he managed to get in contact with Ivanov and Kuzmin, drivers of carrier vehicles. They were both working for the Housing Management authority in Minsk. Blumin met with them many times to figure out a plan for how to escape from the ghetto without getting official documents. Blumin wanted to take weapons out of the ghetto and bring the remaining communists with him. Not wishing to involve any more people than he could avoid, he would meet the drivers personally.

Blumin had a difficult time getting out of the ghetto. Everybody knew him, which made him obvious. His appearance drew people's attention. Nonetheless, the day of the escape was scheduled for the 6th of May 1943. The vehicles, in which Blumin was to leave with his people, arrived in the ghetto: they

---

[39] Awarded by the Nazis for bravery in battle.

[40] The Communist Party was frequently referred to as just "The Party".

were *dushegubkas* full of Gestapo agents. Ivanov was with them. These drove into the ghetto. At 6 o'clock in the morning the neighbourhood where Blumin lived was surrounded. Hitler's murderers knew that Blumin wouldn't hand himself over alive, and so they had brought Epstein with them. Epstein went into Blumin's lodgings and called him, pretending to have come to collect some paperwork on behalf of the Housing Department. Blumin came to the door and a shower of blows from rifle-butts rained down on him. Before he had time to draw breath, he had already fallen to the floor, stunned and bloody. He was unconscious when they tied him up and threw him into the vehicle. His family and all the inhabitants of the block were thrown in with him.

For three weeks the Gestapo tortured Blumin, and for three dark and horrific weeks he survived. For the whole three weeks his torturers would talk to him day and night demanding that he reveal his accomplices, his links and who his sources of weaponry were. In silence, Blumin suffered. In silence he withstood the agony of torture. Not a word or sound came out of his mouth. The brutality and greed of those professional murderers, stripped of any semblance of humanity, was so great that they knocked out his gold tooth filling and kept it for themselves. To make an impression on the rest of the Jews in the ghetto he was put in a vehicle once they had satisfied themselves that nothing useful could be gotten out of him. He was taken to the cemetery in full daylight and shot, and his corpse was thrown into a shared grave. The Jews had trouble recognising the man they had known as Blumin. He had been tall, thickset, and healthy; by the time he was brought to the cemetery he was small, thin, and toothless. The Jews took Blumin's corpse out of the shared grave, buried him in a separate one and paid their respects.

Blumin's sad fate did not stop the Jewish movement for a single minute. Not a day or night passed without people cutting through the wire fence and escaping into the woods. In June 1943 some guides came from one of the partisan detachments asking for medical supplies and a doctor. This responsibility fell to Anna Isaakovna Turetskaya, a very fine doctor and a wonderful comrade and friend. She had once been Head of the orphanage. The children and staff had proudly called her "our mama" and "our Nyuta[41]". She was a beautiful and clever woman. She got on well with everybody and was good at comforting people in hard times, restoring their energy and confidence. She was a shining ray of hope at times when it seemed that dark storm clouds had closed in overhead.

Anna Turetskaya was happy to be called to serve her people. She and her group tried to cross the wire fences four times. Every time she was met with

---

[41] An affectionate nickname form of the proper name 'Anna'.

failure. Either, Epstein and his stooges were guarding the fence, or the Germans were patrolling nearby, or the Polizei were establishing new outposts.

At last, on the night between the 16th and 17th of June 1943 at 11 o'clock the group broke out. At a distance of two kilometres from the ghetto they ran into Scherner, who was leading a detachment of policemen on their way to check the outposts. They attacked the Jews like jackals. The guide was killed, Anna was wounded in the leg and the rest scattered. Now wounded, Anna crawled away and hid in a hole. For three hours the bandits prowled around looking for her. They found her and took her to the 5th police station. They tormented her, beat her up and threw her onto the flagstone floor of the police station. She lay there, covered in cuts and bleeding. Scherner spent hours torturing her, asking her questions in both Russian and German: where she had been going, with whom, what mission was she carrying out. Every word he spoke came with beatings, the blows raining down on her head, shoulders, and injured leg. Scherner stamped on her with his boots. Anna replied that she was not able to understand or answer questions due to the state she was in. Scherner realised that he was not going to get anything out of her.

That morning he dumped her in a vehicle and took her to the Jewish cemetery. She was lifted off her stretcher and carried to the shared grave hole. When they reached it, she began to speak. In answer to Scherner's question "who were you with?" she said: "My whole people were with me. That is who I am saving. You may be about to kill me, but nobody will suffer from it: in fact, after my death even more people will escape and will hate you even more. Look at your hands. There's not a clean patch on them, they're covered in blood. How many children's lives have you ended? I'm not afraid of you. We will be avenged by the whole Soviet people. Go on, kill me." Gathering her last vestiges of strength "Our Nyuta" lifted herself into a sitting position, straightened her back and calmly awaited the bullet. Scherner killed her with a shot from his revolver. Nyuta tumbled off the stretcher into the shared grave, from which some Jews rescued her body and buried it in a separate grave, decorating it with grass and flowers from the fields. The surviving Jews of the Minsk Ghetto will never forget their Nyuta.

From June 1943 the work columns began to be killed. On the 2nd of June 1943, 70 women were gathered with the pretext that they were to be sent to work at the radio factory: 20 were sent to the factory and 50 to the Gestapo. There, they were arranged in lines. Ribbe, surrounded by Gestapo officers, informed his victims that they were about to be loaded into a vehicle and driven out of town to a place where they would be well fed. When the vehicle drove up the women recognised it as one of the *dushegubkas* they were so well acquainted with. The women realised that they were being driven not to work but to their deaths. They started to run, but running from the Gestapo was no easy task and many were shot where they stood, while the rest were forcibly loaded into the vehicle and gassed. Only one of the women, Lilya Kapilovich, managed to escape by hiding under some cars which were parked in the yard. From that time onwards the female labourers began to be systematically killed. Ribbe went around all the firms where there were Jews working and made a record of all of them. After Ribbe's visits the columns disappeared one by one.

September 1943 and the end of the Minsk Ghetto

At the beginning of September 1943 Ribbe appeared in the German Jewish ghetto and selected the 300 youngest and healthiest men. They were loaded into a vehicle like cattle and driven away. A few days later the same thing happened in the Russian Jewish ghetto: two vehicles drove up and men were loaded into them and driven to the camp on Shirokaya Street. A few days after that they were taken away from there too. On the 12th of September 1943 it was announced to the German Jews that they had to prepare to leave for Germany. They began to prepare, hurriedly gathering their essentials, but on the 14th of September instead of being taken to Germany they were loaded into *dushegubkas* and driven away. The German Jewish ghetto ceased to exist, and their lodgings were left empty. The ghetto once again shrank in size.

By the 1st of September 1943 there were only a handful of Jews remaining. On the 21st of October 1943 the ghetto was surrounded by the Gestapo. Once again people were loaded into vehicles and driven away to be killed. In cases where nobody could be found in buildings, grenades were thrown into them, the logic being that anybody hiding in *malinas* would be killed. Dogs were used to help search out the *malinas*.

The Minsk Ghetto ceased to exist. The last Jews died. Not a single stone was left standing in the Minsk Ghetto. Only the ruins were left to keep alive memories of the suffering and torture of days gone by that had been the fate of the Jewish people from the moment that they fell under the yoke of the German occupiers. Over the course of two and a half years the Jews were gradually destroyed. Of the 75,000 Jews left in Minsk when the fascist brutes arrived, by the time this document was created a little over 1,000 were left. In the face of terrible oppression and the threat of death which lay in wait for them at every step, these Jews managed to find a way to break out of the ghetto and escape into the forest to join the partisan detachments.

The rate at which Jews were escaping from the ghetto quickened in April 1943. The Parkhomenko detachment in the Forest[42] and Zorin's national detachment were formed. Zorin knew about the suffering of the ghetto because he had experienced it himself. He organised a national family detachment, systematically sending out guides and accepting everyone into his detachment: the elderly, women, and children. The detachment numbered 600 people.

---

[42] This is referring to Naliboki Forest (in Russian: *"Nalibokskaya Puscha"*).

"Some of the Jews have ended up in battle detachments. Every fighter burns with hatred for the common enemy of all humanity; every fighter carries the vision of ruined cities, villages burnt down, people stripped of all they held dear and children orphaned. Each one carries bleeding wounds, and each of them is striving to deal the enemy the strongest, boldest and hardest blow they can. Now the partisans are coming out of the woods to sever the railway... so one of the enemy's vital arteries, their trains carrying ammunition, equipment and manpower will all fall beneath the swing of the axe. The time when the partisan detachments are to merge with the Red Army is now drawing near."

Anna Machiz,
Naliboki forest,
December 1943

Appendix to the memoirs of Anna Semyonovna Machiz (Levina)

[Editor's note: This appendix reads as a summary text to 'The Minsk Ghetto as Remembered by Anna Machiz']

20.11.1981

Home address: Minsk, Krasnozvyozdnaya Street, Block 1, Flat 4

In August 1941, the communists of the ghetto began to gather in order to resist the enemy and to search each other out. They were finding each other and coming to agreements. 54 of them met for the first time on Ostrovskaya Street. They split responsibilities between them: Weinhaus, a former member of the Council of People's Commissars, had to distribute leaflets. People flocked to the *Judenrat*. "Nays, nays" – give it to us (leaflets, "news"), give it to us, give it to us. Every word of news from the mainland[43] was snatched up and passed on to everybody else. Weinhaus, editor of the leaflets, was killed in a pogrom on the 20th of November.

In the meeting mentioned above the following mandates were issued:

1. Break the mental state of panic prevalent among the Jews.
2. Set up a radio receiver.
3. Systematically release leaflets.
4. Establish contact with the communists in the Russian District.
5. Establish links with the partisan detachments.

Gebelev was tasked with establishing links with the communists of the Russian District. He hid his Russian comrades, who were under threat of being taken to jail, in a *malina* in the ghetto. Reserve lodgings were also created in the Russian District where he could bring communists (Russian Jews). Those fanatics wanted to sow discord between nationalities, but this only unified people. In response to the enemy's machinations the Soviet people became more strongly unified.

---

[43] The "mainland" here literally means "big land" referring to Russia, as Russia was not occupied and was still in the fight. Any news from that front would have been consumed with great interest.

In September 1941 contact was initiated with the Bystrov partisan detachment. This detachment was operating in the western regions of the Republic[44] and it was from here that the first guides came.

The Jewish Committee (or *Judenrat*) was created in the following way. During the first days of the occupation (June 1941) the invaders stopped 10 people in town, took them into the House of Government and made an announcement: "you are to make sure all of our orders are carried out". Those who commit the slightest misdemeanour will be shot. Ilya Mushkin was appointed Chairman (he was the former Deputy Director of Minpromtorg[45]). By the 15th of July 1941, the registration of the Jews of the Minsk Ghetto was completed. Everyone had to wear a yellow patch with the number of the block on which they lived.

A war indemnity was to be levied from the Jews: gold, silver, and Soviet tender. "…Under the leadership of Mushkin (murdered) and Serebryanskiy (police chief, hanged) help was arranged for the partisan detachments: warm clothes, furs, footwear, typewriters, stationery, linen, camouflage suits, socks (my mother knitted them in the basement), bandages, medical supplies, even bread baked in the ghetto bakery – it was guarded by policemen but they still managed to smuggle the bread out. All of this was redirected to the partisan detachments. Mushkin's role was a difficult one. He had to simultaneously give the impression of carrying out the orders of the fascists while in fact doing all that was in his power to help the partisans. Then a traitor blew Mushkin and Serebryanskiy's cover. They were killed. In the pogrom of the 20th of November Weinhaus was killed (this pogrom was a continuation of the one on the 7th of November). "They didn't get enough people" (in the words of the Gestapo) on the 7th of November – so they took another 7000 on the 20th of November. The fearless Weinhaus, a distributor of leaflets who had contacts in the Russian District, died during this pogrom. Under his leadership news summaries were regularly received over the radio to be spread to the ghetto's inhabitants.

The ghetto shrank in size. After pogroms, the streets and buildings that were left vacant in the German Jewish ghetto district were reassigned to the Russian Jewish ghetto district. Pruslin, propaganda secretary of the Voroshilovskiy District Committee, was brought in to replace Weinhaus. At the end of November 1941, a General Party Conference for representatives from the

---

[44] The Republic of Belarus.

[45] The Ministry of Industry and Trade (**Minpromtorg** short for **Ministerstvo promyshlennosti i torgovli**).

Jewish ghetto and communists from the non-Jewish Russian District outside of the ghetto was convened. The representative from the ghetto was Gebelev.

I. Mushkin was arrested in February 1942. He was handed over by the traitors Epstein and Rosenblat. Mushkin was thrown in jail. He spent a long time being tortured and tormented. He was killed while attempting to flee.

From this point onwards, people began to be systematically sent to join the partisan detachments. The general Party conference mandated that a Party organisation should be formed based on the principle of *"desyatkas"*. *Desyatkas* were formed via personal connections and recommendations. Every secretary of a *desyatka* was linked to a higher figure of authority in his or her zone. There were four zones in total. The ghetto was one of the designated zones.

Thanks to connections with the members of the *Judenrat* it proved possible to assign people to work on sites where they could obtain weaponry. Feldman undertook the search for weaponry. He was betrayed, but the Nazis didn't know which Feldman to search for. Ioffe, the newly appointed Chairman of the *Judenrat, gave* no-one away. People continued to pour into work columns and gain access to sites where they could source weaponry.

Helped by workers of the *Judenrat* and the service for public order, people were redirected into "skilled worker" columns so as to get them onto work sites. The call to "arm yourselves!" was circulated. Trade was carried out by the wire perimeter of the ghetto, and policemen were bought off with watches, gold coins and suits. People felt more confident once they were armed and had a way to resist and take revenge on the hated enemy. Mikhail Ruditskiy, a stonemason, obtained a rifle. Baum, a tailor who laboured in a workshop belonging to the German police, always kept a large pair of scissors at hand so as to put them to good use when the opportunity presented itself.

Mikhail Gebelev went off to the Russian District for a meeting at which a mandate was given to create a large net of Party groups in which the ghetto was included as one of the zones. The Party conference effectively created an Underground Party committee. Its secretary was "Slavik". The authority in charge of the municipal Party committee was Smolar (he was residing in the ghetto under the surname of Stolyarevich) whose Party nickname was "Modest". The heating plant at the Jewish hospital served as a headquarters from which Smolar operated. Here the communists gathered and the most serious and pressing issues were discussed and brought to attention.

The heads of the *desyatkas* were: Naum Feldman, Zyama Okun, Nadya Schusser, Maizels, Rolbin, Rubenchik. Emma Rodova, a member of the

Komsomol, was appointed as signaller for contact with the communists in the Russian District. The following tasks were assigned to the *desyatkas*.

1. Nominate candidates from among the communists and combat-ready individuals to be sent off to the communist partisan detachments.
2. Gather weaponry.
3. Send material support to the partisan detachments in the form of warm clothes.
4. Gather and send medical supplies to the partisan detachments.
5. Create a fund to help the needy. Connect with the Russian non-Jewish population.

Thanks to links with Soviet members of the *Judenrat*, it proved possible to position people where they could be most effective in the fight against the fascists. A group of young people were sent to work sites. A centre of command was assigned.

The ghetto got its chance to send people off to the partisan detachments. The task was as follows: to select the most combat-ready individuals, trained in warfare, to go about energetically gathering weaponry and medical supplies, and to prepare doctors to send off to the detachments, as well as to create a fund to support ghetto prisoners who were starving.

The greater part of the war indemnity levied from prisoners of the ghetto was actually syphoned off by the Municipal Party Committee for the needs of the partisan detachments.

Then there was the matter of creating a shared printing press for the whole city. Printing sorts[46], typewriters, radio apparatus and weaponry were obtained. All of this was sent out to the detachments. Zyama Okun undertook to organise the underground printing press. A group of people were successfully rescued from the concentration camp on Shirokaya Street. They reached the detachment on carts and horses, having packed many useful items to bring with them. A double bottom was made to hide the weapons before setting off in the direction where they reasoned that the detachments would be located. On their approach to Kalvariya they met Kudryakov (a true patriot of his homeland), and he showed them where the weapons were hidden. They dug up 13 rifles and 4000 rounds out of the ground.

Another group of 20 people arrived from the ghetto. The commander of the detachment gave the order to send for another party of people from the

---

[46] The individual letter blocks used in printing presses.

ghetto immediately, saying: "Anyone who wants to fight against our bloodthirsty enemy should come and join the ranks of the partisans."

Meanwhile the shootings of the 20th and 22nd of December 1941 continued on the city's streets (Moskovskaya, Sovetskaya and Pushkinskaya streets). There were corpses lying everywhere; people were not allowed to clear them away.

Messengers from the city would come to the ghetto, get in contact with the *Judenrat* and receive warm clothes, footwear, medical supplies, soap and money and they would then transfer these items to the partisan detachments via the town committee.

A directive was received: to unify all of the fighting groups in the ghetto.

In February 1942 the *desyatkas* in the ghetto which were transferring people to the detachments numbered 12 in total. Misha Gebelev undertook the business of building contacts outside the ghetto and Pruslin was in charge of coordinating propaganda[47]. Nina Liss carried out tasks outside the ghetto and was equipped with a fake passport under a Belarusian identity[48]. She organised people to be sent to the detachments. Khasya Bindler operated as a diplomatic courier. She maintained links with the *Judenrat*.

Gebelev, Anya (surname unknown), Klara Zheleznyak – Gorelik, Berta Libo - via the aforementioned women, Gebelev maintained contact with his comrades in the Russian District.

Mirkin arranged for members of his *desyatka* to work in a German institution where they could obtain ammunition. In the terrifying environment of the ghetto, they became skilled at sneaking out beyond the wire fence and choosing suitable people to send off to join the detachments.

Kagan fully armed his group with pistols and revolvers. Naum Brustin's *desyatka* had fifteen grenades. Yosif Mendel gathered an arsenal of weaponry

---

[47] The word 'propaganda' used here in Russian doesn't have the same negative connotations as the English word 'propaganda' of misleading information designed to indoctrinate its target audience. 'Organising propaganda' here means something more like 'organising communications to bolster morale', much as the British government did as part of its own war effort.

[48] Under the Soviet Union (and the Russian Empire), "Jewish" was considered to be a nationality, separate to "Belarusian" or "Russian" etc. One could not be both.

stored at the cemetery. Feldman would buy weapons from the Germans[49] and bring them to a "storeroom" on Respublikanskaya Street.

Rolbin hid six rifles and several hundred rounds in a hole dug within the ghetto itself. He established links with some Belarusian comrades. Valik Zhitelzey and Nonna Markevich hid 30 rifles and a large amount of ammunition in a hole dug outside the wire fence. Their group got out of the ghetto working together with their Belarusian comrades Vitya Rudovich and Kolya Prischepkin. They located and dug up 540 rounds, a machine gun belt and 2 grenades in the district of the Mogilev highroad. The call went out to obtain weaponry by any means.

Abram Helman, a tailor, stole a brand-new machine gun from the German police's stores. Layba Shafran obtained a Maxim gun from the peat factory where he worked just outside Minsk. Doctors Kulik, Minkin and others helped the resistance to get their hands on medical supplies. The fearless and tireless Misha Gebelev was arrested at the wire fence. He was shot.

The prisoner of war, Semyon Grigoryevich Gazenko, who had organised an escape from the camp on Shirokaya Street, made it to one of the detachments. A detachment was created and named after Budyonny. The Commissar of the detachment was Feldman. The detachment was added to the Stalin brigade.

It was decided that an underground printing press should be created in the ghetto. Misha Arotsker, Kaplan (himself a printer), Lena Maizelis and Andrei Ivanovich Podoprigora brought the printing sorts from the Russian District. Abram Tunik (who was gravely injured in battle) supplied the radio receiver. Information about the situation on the front was printed and disseminated. Emma Rodova, David Hertzik, Dora Berson and Nonna Markevich listened to operative summaries over the radio receiver and passed them on to the ghetto's inmates.

Contact with the partisan detachments in the Radoshkovichi district was sought via Vovka (surname unknown). Vovka managed to make contact. Schedletskiy was the first messenger from the partisan detachment. He was awarded three Orders and medals for his actions. For us, now trapped in the ghetto, it was heartening to hear that the partisans were doing battle with our bloodthirsty enemy, the fascists. And any route out of the ghetto invariably led to the partisan detachments.

---

[49] In some instances, German soldiers were known to sell weapons to Jews.

Weaponry and medical supplies continued to be gathered. We asked the detachments' command to help us smuggle people out of the ghetto. The detachments kept changing location and frequently slipped out of contact. The Frunze brigade was formed from three detachments (Frunze, Dzerzhinskiy and Sergey Lazo). From the 1st of February 1943 the mass extermination of the ghetto's inmates began.

Contact was initiated with the Stalin and Chkalov brigades and the Budyonny detachment. Commander Semyon Ganzenko sent some children who were in the detachment to guide people out of the ghetto. 12-year-old Benya (surname unknown) died a heroic death fighting the bloodthirsty fascists having successfully led over 100 people out of the ghetto. Davidka Klionskiy made 12 trips to the ghetto to guide people out. Fanya Gimpel guided some doctors out who brought medical supplies with them.

Tsilya Klebanova, a partisan from the Kutuzov detachment, came to the ghetto from her detachment six times and brought people back every time. Tsilya Klebanova and Bronya Goldman set off for the ghetto one last time but this time they found it empty. It had already been liquidated by the fascist brutes.

There were no limits to the atrocities committed by the fanatics Ribbe, Michelson, Bunge and Scherner: whether a child was found with a piece of German bread, a piece of butter was taken to feed a child or a patch was sewn on wrongly – the punishment was that you would be shot. The poor children would squeeze under the wire fence to get into the Russian District where they would be fed a little and be given food to take back. The children tried to return to the ghetto with the work columns, but these little children would be laughed at and shot.

Yefim Rosenblat, a thief and drunkard from Warsaw who served the fascist scum with his heart and soul, was made head of the Labour Market and Chief of the Jewish Militia. He handed over communists and tracked down members of the underground and spied on them. He had the blood of many Soviet citizens on his hands. However, for some reason Ribbe was not satisfied with him. He removed Rosenblat by sending him to jail where he was shot in February 1943.

Ribbe appointed Yefim Epstein to replace Rosenblat. In Ribbe's own words, he trusted him more. He clearly knew his man: Epstein and his pack of wolves, which included Elinka Ginzburg, Mulya Kagan, and Mira Markman, organised nighttime pogroms. Yet even these vermin realised that they could not hold on to power for long. Some were tricked into going to meet one of the [partisan] detachments; the people's sentence was unanimous: "they must be shot!" This sentence was duly fulfilled. Negotiations were also attempted with Epstein, but he wouldn't go into the forest. He thought that the German fanatics would spare him, but he was wrong.

During one nighttime pogrom when atrocities were being committed, a block was surrounded and the German fascists demanded to be given Losik (a member of the underground), but he happened not to be at home. At that time, he was buying up weaponry from the German stores in *Krasnoye* Urochische. The block was blown up, but they managed to hide the weaponry which Losik had obtained. People were taken outside wearing only their nightclothes and shot dead on the spot. On the 31st of March 1943 a chain of men surrounded the house where Nina Liss lived. Tulskiy, a *provokator*, M. Gebelev and N. Feldman went and hid in a *malina* and Yefim Stolyarevich hid in the hospital. On the 20th of April 1942 the block on Kollektornaya Street where Naum Brustin lived was surrounded. He was killed along with all the inhabitants of that block. The radio receiver was tracked down. Grenades were thrown into the block. The people who lived there were killed and the building was destroyed.

Besides sending people to join the partisan detachments, the idea of carrying out sabotage missions at work sites where people from the ghetto were labouring was raised. Lena Maizels, Fanya Gurvich, Fanya Chepik, Lena Pevsner, and others worked at *Bolshevik*, a factory. They deliberately damaged items made of leather, destroyed some of the parachutes and stole linen and mittens. The male group stole several field telephones from the factory. The group which included Silberstein, Shapiro, Grichannik, Sukenik and others was tasked with the following mission: to delay the completion of orders, spoil raw and processed materials and expend as much raw material as possible. Shoemakers labouring on work sites put huge amounts of nails into the soles of the boots they were making. Made this way, the boots were impossible to put on. Tailors on work sites would sew right-handed sleeves onto the left side of garments and vice versa. Hitler's cut-throats could not handle their harsh Russian surroundings without spirits to drink, but labourers working at the distillery did a poor job of distilling spirits so that it would give little pleasure to the fascist scum drinking it on the war front.

Schultz (a German) smuggled 37 people out of the ghetto to one of the detachments.

Contact was initiated with railway workers; they would hide people trying to join the partisan detachments in steam trains. They would transport them to the zone where the detachments were. Over 500 people were smuggled out this way.

The issue of smuggling children out of the ghetto into orphanages located in the Russian District was raised and this plan had partial success thanks to links with Soviet members of the Municipal Board. Anna Turetskaya, a doctor at the orphanage, said these words when she was taken to the cemetery to be shot: "I'm not afraid of you. Shoot me! Our soldiers will come and avenge us." They shot her. She tumbled into the shared grave. Some Jews rescued her body and buried it in a separate grave.

On the instruction of the commanders of the partisan detachments stationed in the Naliboki Forest, ghetto inmates (the elderly, women, and children) were smuggled out to join the detachments under various pretexts. A family detachment numbering 600 people was organised. A fighting group was formed within this detachment which did battle with the enemy, thwarting their efforts on the railways and highroads.

Printers, weaponry experts and doctors were sent to join other detachments, including the author of this memoir – Anna Machiz, former investigator for top-priority cases of the Office of the Public Prosecutor of the BSSR – who was sent to work in the special department of the Zhukov Brigade.

The initial memoirs were written in December 1943 in the partisan detachment. The document notes that the text was prepared and written down in the partisan detachment in December 1943.

Due to the originality, importance, and format of the author's material, during the preparation of this publication by the compiler and editor it was left without alterations[50].

Commentary and explanations of the text have not been provided due to the fact that numerous academic publications and literature, which treat the history of the Minsk Ghetto, already contain guides to the terms used and the names referring to people and geographical locations which appear. Our material is meant to be read by historians, specialists and anybody interested in the subject of Holocaust history, the German occupation, and the organisation of the underground and partisan movement within Belarus. The compilation of this text, written in 1981, was undertaken by Oksana Yankovich, an expert advisor of the Historical Workshop (note from ed. – K.K.).

---

[50] Minor edits were made in the translation from Russian to English.

Section 3

Supporting publications and documents

This section contains publications and documents, which feature excerpts from Anna Machiz's diary and her memoirs, which were posted in periodicals (newspapers, magazines) and academic articles.

Publications

Anna Machiz - from The Ninth Circle, by Guy David Pp. 51-52, 79-81.[51]

Just my luck: I ran into both of them on the same day.

Serebryanskiy shot out from around a corner with his assistants and loomed in front of me. It was too late to run. I froze. Although I knew that he was in the ghetto and this encounter might happen, I realised that inwardly I hadn't been prepared for it. Naturally, I didn't give away that I knew him. He too flinched and turned the other way.

Zyama Serebryanskiy had lived not far from us before the war; our mothers knew each other. Ironically enough I, an investigator for the Public Prosecutor of Belarus, had taken part in legal proceedings against him and his brother. It was a case of embezzled state funds. Via my mother the brothers tried to convince me to help them avoid court. Needless to say, nothing came of this.

Serebryanskiy was freed after serving his sentence five days before the war began. In the ghetto, he commanded the Jewish service for public order; at the slightest provocation he would begin to shout, waving his stick or whip – he and his "operatives" were not entrusted with real weaponry. And now I, a communist and former investigator, had crossed his line of vision.

If only this day could be over. But no. Someone else saw me in the yard beneath our residential block, someone who I had previously taken to court, also for embezzlement: Monisov the cashier. I was actually far less wary of him than of Zyama – he didn't wield the same power; he and I were in an identical position.

Inside our block everything was a bustle and there was commotion. Where should I run to get away from Serebryanskiy, where could I hide? As we deliberated, a girl I knew arrived: a former student at the faculty of law whom I had once taken on for work experience. She beckoned me to one side. "Anna Semyonovna, I have a message for you from Serebryanksiy. He asked me to tell you that he won't abuse his power no matter what and that if there's anything

---

[51] This appears to be a mistake in the original text: David Guy was author of a book about the Minsk Ghetto titled *Desyaty Krug* (*The Tenth Circle*); there is only one letter difference in Russian between "Ninth" and "Tenth". This book was also released in America under the title of *Innocence in Hell*.

that you ever need, to let him know so that he can help, because he is an upright Soviet and has no intention of getting back at you."

So that was that. I discovered later that Zyama was linked to the communists in the ghetto and was aiding the partisans by supplying clothes and weaponry to their detachments. He would inform people before there were due to be *actions* giving many people the chance to try and hide. The mean act he put on was just for show.

Monisov, on the other hand, gave me a fair share of trouble…

He would slink from house to house, sniffing me out, leaving no corner unsearched. I had to find a new hiding place every night. Then he denounced me to the SD. The *Judenrat* received an inquiry. "Where is Machiz? Bring her to the Gestapo." They dug around in the card-index and then replied: "She is absent from our records." The thing is that I had registered with the *Judenrat* under a maiden name[52]. What happened after that? After that, Monisov was taken during a raid and killed. At that point I stopped hiding.

The ghetto was like that: some people were still human and respected law and order. Others, finding themselves at death's door, tried to settle old scores. True, shared misfortunes bring people together, but they can also drive a wedge between them: one must look this unpleasant truth in the face. There are people who start to think only about saving their own skin. Then the lower instincts creep out from beneath the surface.

"While eating lunch, he would casually remark between the soup course and the vegetable course "I want to kill all the Jews in Europe. This war is the decisive struggle between National Socialism and Jews the world over. One of the two will be destroyed, and it will definitely not be us.""

From the memoirs of Speer,
a Nazi criminal, about Hitler

Life in the ghetto went on – not that it could really be called life; it was some kind of undefinable thing, a particular type of captivity that bred despair. Nonetheless, many people began to ask themselves the blindingly obvious question: *How should one act in order to avoid being killed? Simply sit around doing nothing and wait for God knows what, flinching at every small sound of*

---

[52] She most likely means her mother's maiden name – Svinovskaya.

movement, diving into malinas in panic at the slightest sign that the Germans are about to appear?

Some data suggests that there were around three hundred communists and *Komsomol* members in the ghetto; others make the figure significantly larger. But what does it matter how many there were? There were others who tried everything to hide their pre-war past, as it was precisely these kinds of people that the Gestapo would seek out and mercilessly destroy. Still others started to scrutinise and size up the people around them, and so by degrees the resistance began to brew.

At the very end of 1942, 53 Jews from the city of Slutsk arrived in the Minsk Ghetto. They had been brought in as "skilled workers." They told stories of the gradual liquidation of the ghetto in Slutsk and would often mention Ribbe, an officer of the Gestapo notable for his exceptional cruelty.

At the beginning of January two unknown figures appeared in the ghetto. Their clothes bore the distinguishing marks of the Gestapo. One day while walking down the street they stopped a woman, searched her, confiscated the eight stamps which they found on her and carried on walking.

Another Jewish woman with her four-year-old son crossed their path. They stopped her and asked why she was not at work. The woman presented a note giving her exemption. At this the two of them attacked her, beat her up and dragged her to the cemetery, where they shot her.

On their way back from the cemetery they came across a boy about fifteen years old carrying two chunks of firewood. They asked him: "Where did you get the wood?" He replied: "My boss gave it to me at work." They dragged him to the cemetery as well and murdered him.

The two Gestapo agents continued their rampage until the evening. Coming home with the work columns, the Slutsk Jews recognised them: "That's Ribbe with his translator Michelson. They must be starting the liquidation of the ghetto."

Ribbe and his pack of wolves tirelessly patrolled the ghetto breaking into homes. It was even worse than a mass pogrom. If they found a German roll of bread: death by firing squad; a slab of butter for a sick child: death by firing squad; a map or a Soviet book: death by firing squad.

It was Ribbe who came up with the idea of a carnival. It is possible that he visited one while inspecting the work columns of the German Jews, who were very different from the local ones. We had been thoroughly crushed, but they still retained some semblance of humanity.

One day Ribbe took a walk along the work columns on their way back to the ghetto. He personally selected twelve of the most beautiful women who had come from Germany. None of the others satisfied his refined taste. He chose one woman from Minsk to add to them: Lina Neu. Ribbe ordered for them to be gathered at the Labour Market at ten o'clock the following day, and for there to be an equal number of Jewish operatives "strong workers" – young good-looking ones.

At the appointed time he drove up to the Labour Market and ordered each of the young "operatives" to take a beautiful lady by the arm and to proceed from the Labour Market down Sukhaya Street at a slow, steady, and orderly pace. There was a groan as someone realised what this meant: they were going to the cemetery. The pairs moved off one after another, just like at a carnival. Ribbe watched to make sure they weren't hurrying and that the intervals between each pair were maintained. When they reached the gates to the cemetery one woman asked permission to say goodbye to her husband. Ribbe agreed to this. Her husband was sent for. They arrived at the cemetery and stopped. A Gestapo officer ordered the "operatives" to strip the women naked. Some of them were crying and one screamed: "I want to live!"

"Cavaliers, invite your ladies to waltz! Don't be shy! Take them by the waist, gently and humbly, and let's begin..." commanded Ribbe. The "operatives" led the women in a dance. Ribbe sang a melody from *the Vienna Woods*, conducting with his right hand, which was holding a pistol. The "operatives" picked up melody and the pairs began to twirl...

Meanwhile, the husband whom the woman had asked to say goodbye to had been brought. The waltz came to a halt. Ribbe allowed them to embrace and kiss each other, and then immediately ordered for the husband to be shot. The crying intensified. Ribbe lined the beautiful women up separately, took out a pistol and methodically shot them. Michelson helped finish them off with his own gun. On his way out of the cemetery Ribbe picked up somebody's bra. He toyed with it for a bit and then put it in his pocket. "To remind me of a beautiful Jewish girl," he said offhand as he walked away. Ribbe gradually liquidated the ghetto. Methodically, punctually, and with know-how.

From June 1943 the work columns began to be killed. At the radio factory seventy women were selected. Fifty of them were sent to the Gestapo. Ribbe lined them up in the yard and announced: "You will now be loaded into a vehicle and driven out of town to a workplace where you will be well fed." The vehicle drove up. The women could see that it was a *dushegubka* – a mobile gas chamber. Succumbing to instinct they began to flee in all directions, but the Gestapo could not be outrun. All of them were shot. Lilya Kapilovich alone managed to escape by hiding.

The remnants of the "Hamburg" Jews were liquidated via a farcical procedure. They were told a wonderful fairy tale: they were going home. These Jews packed their essentials. Next stop was in fact the *dushegubka*.

Fleeing into the forest, where partisan detachments were operating, was the only escape. Anyone who was still able to stand on two feet tried this, whether old or young, accompanied by guides or alone. They ran wherever their feet took them, thinking only of breaking out from the hated wire fence.

Picture a group photograph: two people in civilian clothes and the rest in jackets. All of them are decorated with medals and awards. Their lips are drawn back slightly in a hint of a smile: it is obvious that the photograph was taken at the very end of the war, and however much the people posing in it wanted to remain pointedly serious in a manner befitting the occasion, their lips betray the joy they are feeling. They are the Commissar of the Lazo detachment, the Commissar of the 208th detachment, the Commissar of the 25th Anniversary of the BSSR detachment, the Commander of the sabotage unit of the Budyonny detachment, the Commissar of the 106th detachment… Yefim Stolyarevich, Boris Khaimovich, Naum Feldman, Vladimir Kravchinskiy and Yefim Feigelman: all escapees from the Minsk Ghetto.

I came across this photo[53] while acquainting myself with a lengthy publication recounting stories of concentration camps and ghettos during the war. The years of Hitlerism produced a fair amount of this material, hence the weightiness of the publication. It first saw the light on German soil in the German Democratic Republic[54]. The Minsk Ghetto got a fair share of attention, being one of the largest in Europe.

Its former inmates became avengers who fought in many different detachments. Members of the ghetto's underground were directly involved in the creation of at least seven detachments. The 106th was fully Jewish.

---

[53] Leonid Tsyrinskiy never had this photo and therefore it was not available to be included in this book.

[54] Commonly known as East Germany.

From the 1981 memoirs by former inmate of the Minsk Ghetto Anna Machiz

...medical supplies and weaponry continued to be gathered. We began asking the command of the partisan detachments to help smuggle people out of the ghetto. The detachments would change location and we often lost contact with them. It was mainly children who guided people out of the ghetto as it was easier for them to get past the guards. These were 12-year-old Benya (I could not confirm his surname) who successfully led over 100 people out of the ghetto (he died a brave man's death), Davidka Klionskiy who made 12 trips to the ghetto to guide people out, Fanya Gimpel who guided some doctors out who brought medical supplies with them, 10-year-old Lyonya Okun, Tsilya Klebanova, Sima Fiterson and many others. They were all heroes, as the Nazis were trying to track them down and would have shot on sight too.

National Archives of the Republic of Belarus
Quoted from a copy in the archive of Yad Vashem. M-41 (2), sheet 7.)

A contemporary of the war[55]

From an interview by Alena Dzyadzyudya with Leonid Tsyrinskiy // Zvyazda[56]. 30th June 2011

This year Leonid Tsyrinskiy turned 70. Truth be told, for him the war represents the worst memories of his mother and his own worst memories: even ten or so years after victory was won, he was still dreaming of Germans in their home.

"My mother would anticipate the 22nd of June every year with terror. She was afraid that the same thing would happen again. Imagine the scene: a young woman with a month-old baby in her arms, beside her a six-year-old daughter, the war going on all around, and her walking from Rudensk to Minsk on foot," Leonid Tsyrinskiy relates. "To begin with we were in the Rudensk Ghetto, and when we got wind of a pogrom about to happen, we left for Minsk. After we left Minsk, my mother obtained documents which stated that she was not a Jew. I was an eight-month-old baby, and my mother carried me through the

---

[55] This passage was originally in Belarusian, not Russian.

[56] A Belarusian newspaper: its name means The Star. Unlike the rest of the book, the whole of this interview with Leonid Tsyrinskiy is in the Belarusian language.

bitter frosts[57] in her arms and in this way, we came to the village of Valoki. It is no wonder the memory made her fret, because in the summer of 1942 she tripped and cut her calf on a rusty wire while running away from the Germans. That wound never healed right up to her death. I could also mention the post-war years when she worked on her own to feed herself and two children, earning a wage of 19 roubles a month (at that time a loaf of bread cost about 30 roubles and wheat flour bread cost about 80 roubles). After the war, when she was looking for employment, she had to fill out a form asking where she had been during the war. If my mother had written that she had been in occupied territory she would not have been accepted to work – not even as a cashier! Our auntie was a lawyer, so she taught her what to write: "I was in a partisan-held zone."

"And in your opinion, is the war still unknown and a mystery to this day?" I enquire.

"It wasn't the done thing to tell stories about it. People didn't talk about it at home with their families. We are only now beginning to understand the full horror of what happened, and maybe we'll never fully understand it. My sister was 6 years old when the war began, and she saw children's heads being bashed against tanks. She experienced all of that horror and for her the war never ended. I brought her the documents that you had to sign to receive compensation for somebody who had been hiding in occupied territory (she was living alone and could have used the money) but she tore up the documents, and now the war is a taboo topic between us.

Perhaps, so that this doesn't happen again, younger generations should be told more stories about the war? A truthful portrait of the war still needs to be painted.

Alena Dzyadzyudya // Zvyazda[58]. 30th June 2011

---

[57] The original Belarusian uses the adjective *'voda khryschenskaya'* (literally: 'baptismal') to describe the frosts. In the Orthodox Church the baptism of Christ is celebrated on the 6th of January. Within living memory, the temperature in Belarus used to sometimes drop to around minus 40 degrees Celsius at this time of year.

[58] A Belarusian newspaper: its name means *The Star*. Unlike the rest of the book, the whole of this interview with Leonid Tsyrinskiy is in the Belarusian language.

Documents

Order from the Field Commandant's office to create a ghetto in Minsk

Minsk
19th July 1941

A designated part of the city of Minsk shall hereby be allocated solely for the resettlement of Jewish people.

All of the Jewish population of the city of Minsk are to move to the Jewish district within 5 days of the publication of this order. Any Jews encountered outside the Jewish district after this deadline will be arrested and severely punished.

Those being resettled shall be allowed to bring their personal possessions with them. Persons caught trying to export or steal possessions not belonging to them will be shot on sight.

The Jewish district is confined to the following streets: Kolkhozniy Lane, Kolkhoznaya Street, the River Svisloch, Nemiga Street excluding the Orthodox church, Respublikanskaya Street, Shornaya Street, Kollektornaya Street, Mebelniy Lane, Perekopskaya Street, Nizovaya Street, the Jewish cemetery, Obuvnaya Street, 2nd Opanskiy lane, Zaslavlskaya [sic] Street up to Kolkhozniy Lane.

Once the resettlement is complete the Jewish residential district is to be enclosed with a stone wall and fenced off from the rest of the city. The wall is to be built by the residents of the Jewish district. For this purpose, bricks from non-residential buildings and buildings allotted for destruction shall be used.

Jewish people assigned to work teams are forbidden to stay outside the Jewish district. Work teams may leave the Jewish district only with a special pass [official document] to the workplace, issued by the administrative board of Minsk. Anyone violating this order is to be shot.

Cont'd

Jews may only enter and exit the ghetto via Opanskiy and Ostrovskaya Streets. Climbing over the wall is forbidden. German security and the auxiliary police have been given the order to fire on persons violating this order.

Access to the Jewish district is permitted only for Jews, servicemen from German military units with official business there and members of the administrative board of Minsk.

A loan of 30,000 *chervontsy* shall be given to the Jewish Council to cover expenses associated with the resettlement. This sum, the interest on which will be settled at a later date, is to be transferred to the Administrative Board's pay office on 28 Karl Marx Street within 12 hours of the publication of this order.

The Jewish Council is to immediately provide the Housing Department with details of all Jewish properties left outside the Jewish district which are not yet occupied by the Aryan (non-Jewish) population.

Law and order in the Jewish residential district shall be upheld by special Jewish squads, a decree for the creation of which will be issued in due course.

The Jewish Council of the city of Minsk bears responsibility for the complete resettlement of the Jewish population into the allocated district. Any violation of this order shall be met with severe punishment.

NARB [National Archive of the Republic of Belarus]. F. [file] 4683. Op. [special folder] 3. D. [document] 937. L. [sheet] 6-7; F. 359. Op. 1. D. 8. L. 1-2.

From Communiqué No. 31 of the Security Police and the SD on the creation of the Jewish Council (*Judenrat*)

> *Minsk*
> *23rd July 1941*
>
> Solving the Jewish Question while at war on this territory seems to be an unachievable aim since, due to the huge number of Jews, it is only possible to solve it through their resettlement. However, to create a more or less suitable basis for action for the foreseeable future, the following measures have been taken by Einsatzgruppe "B" throughout the area where it has executed its duties so far.
>
> In every city a temporary Chairman of the Jewish Council has been appointed and tasked with the creation of a Jewish Council numbering 3 to 10 people. The Jewish Council will bear total responsibility for the behaviour of the Jewish population. In addition to this it is to begin the registration of all Jews residing within the locality without delay. Furthermore, the Jewish Council is to create labour groups from a number of Jews of ages 15 to 55 who are to work on clearing debris in the city and on other jobs for German institutions and military units. Female Jewish groups of the same ages are being created as well.
>
> Since the German soldier is not capable of unfailingly distinguishing Jews from the non-Jewish local population and misunderstandings have arisen in some cases, an order has been issued throughout the city with immediate effect requiring that Jewish men and women over the age of 10 wear yellow patches sewn onto the chests and backs of their clothes.
>
> The Jewish Council is to report to the city's temporary Commissars. Trustworthy Belarusians selected and suggested by the Einsatzkommando have been appointed to the post of City Commissar.
>
> The foremost and hardest problem to solve in connection with the huge number of Jews is how to accommodate them within the ghetto. This task is already underway. Together with the field and local commandants' offices, city neighbourhoods suitable for the purpose have now been selected.

Cont'd

Due to destruction and pillaging, economic activity was initially paralysed. Some work sites in Minsk and Borisov are now being returned to function. Due to requisitions and thieving agricultural production has been compromised, and this has seriously weakened the supply of food to the population. For the moment, money has no practical purpose in this context and wages are being paid in bread.

Total agreement and unanimity have been reached with the commander of the rear group of the army on the matter of how partisans and former soldiers wearing civilian clothes should be dealt with.

Mass operations involving the security police and the SD have been initiated. They will be conducted without mercy.

On 14.07.1941 the destruction of 4234 people was reported. On 19.07.1941 the number of people liquidated rose by another 3386.

National Archive of the Republic of Belarus. F. 4683. Op. 3. Document. 943. Sheet. 88-89. Translated from German.

From Operative Summary No. 92 of the Security Police and the SD on the execution of an annihilation campaign in the Minsk Ghetto

23rd September 1941

Belorussia:

...combing out the Minsk Ghetto. In cooperation with the Security Service Police and with the help of the field gendarmerie a major campaign has been led in the ghetto. Around 2500 Jews have been arrested including women. Over the course of 3 days 2278 of these have been executed.

The people referred to here are exclusively saboteurs and Jewish activists. It is also to be noted that many of them were not wearing the required distinguishing symbols on their clothes.

NARB. F. 4683. Op. 3. D. 1065. L. 190; MKF. Arch. [archive] No. 175, K. 72379-72380. Translated from German.

Order No. 24 of the commandant of Belorussia on the destruction of Jews and Gypsies

Minsk
24th November 1941

...Jews and Gypsies: orders No. 9 of 28.09.1941, p. 6; No. 11 of 04.10.1941 p. 2. v, No. 13 of 10.10.41, p. 18. As stipulated in these orders: the Jews must disappear from the face of the earth, and the gypsies must likewise be destroyed. Conducting operations on a larger scale against the Jewish People is not the task of this detachment's units. Operations are being carried out by Civil and Police units as per the order of the Commandant of Belorussia if special units are transferred to his jurisdiction... Small groups of Jews may be destroyed or transferred to the ghetto, where they will then be subject to civil administration or the SD.

Baron von Bechtolsheim

NARB. F. 378. Op. 1. D. 698. L. 32. Translation from German.

From Communiqué No. 178 of the Security Police and the SD on anti-Jewish actions in Minsk

Minsk
9th March 1942

Commander Hoffmann ordered a major Aktion against Russian Jews of both sexes to be carried out in Minsk and Koidanov between the 1st and 3rd of March. In order to keep the aforementioned event a secret the *Judenrat* was informed that 5000 Jews were to be "resettled" from the ghetto and that they should be selected by the *Judenrat* and gathered ready for departure. Each Jew could bring 5 kg of luggage. The true purpose of the Chief of the Security Police and the SD was kept a secret. When the ghetto was surrounded on the morning of the 1st of March 1942, not a single Jew was presented by the *Judenrat* for departure. For this reason, detachments were put into action in order to clear part of the ghetto of Jews. Only after this were some Jews gathered and sent in the direction of Minsk-Tovarnaya Station in a long column. Many people did not leave their residences willingly or attempted to avoid being sent away. Force was used to deal with these people and some of them were shot where they stood. After the cleansing of the ghetto many corpses were left lying indoors and outdoors which were later cleared away. At the station people were loaded into wagons which were then joined to one long train which was sent to Koidanov, a small town 30 km to the south-west of Minsk on the Minsk-Baranovichi-Brest-Litovsk railway line.

The next day, the 2nd of March 1942, all the subdivisions of the security police and the SD set off to execute the passengers on the train. A lot of trenches had been prepared for this campaign near Koidanov. To begin with the Jews were unloaded from the wagons and then split into small groups which were led to the trenches by Lithuanian guards. Force was used. Here they were ordered to remove their coats and outerwear. This was done to make shooting them easier. Then the Jews were ordered to walk along the trenches, near to which stood gunmen armed with pistols. The team of gunmen numbered 10-20 people. Each gunman would periodically choose a victim whom he would order to stop, or physically stop with one hand. If the victim was conveniently placed the soldier shot him or her in the back of the head. If after being shot the person did not fall into the trench, he or she was pushed or thrown in.

Cont'd

The trenches were wide, long, and deep enough to fit many hundreds of corpses at minimum.

Groups of Jews standing far away from the trenches could hear the shots and may have realised that a mass execution had begun and that they would be its next victims. Later, when they saw the trenches and the corpses lying in them, it became clear at least to the adults what fate awaited them. Many tried to run, screamed, or cried, but most gave themselves up to their fate without wailing or lamentation. There was no doctor to pronounce the bodies dead. However, care was taken to fire extra shots into bodies that were still moving or if the gunmen had any suspicions that someone was still alive.

The operation that day was not successful in shooting all the people necessary. For this reason, the execution was extended to the 3rd of March 1942. All in all, no fewer than 3 thousand people were killed. How many were killed on the 2nd of March and how many on the 3rd of March was not established, but it is clear that no fewer than 1000 were shot.

According to Communiqué No. 178 of the 9th of March 1942, during the campaign led in Minsk-Koidanov on the 2nd - 3rd of March, 3412 Jews were shot.

...The campaign led in Minsk against the Jews on 03.03.1942 gave the city's population reason to suppose that in the subsequent weeks even bigger campaigns would be conducted against the Jews across the whole of Belorussia.

Federal archive of Koblenz 9ks/62. Matters of justice and Nazi crimes. T. 19. Current No. 552. Photocopy. Translated from German.

From the review of the Commissar of the criminal police Obersturmführer Burckhardt on the position of the German Jews in the Minsk Ghetto

Minsk, 1942

The 7000 German Jews brought to the Minsk Ghetto constitute a particular problem in solving the Jewish problem. These Jews have been accommodated in various parts of the ghetto and in accordance with the wishes of the General Commissariat they have been fenced off from districts inhabited by Russian Jews with barbed wire. So, it has transpired that the German Jews are now not only surrounded by a barbed wire barrier, but also fenced off from the Russian ones, and the rest of the ghetto has not yet totally been surrounded with a wire fence.

Although there are fewer skilled workers amongst the German Jews, taking into account their knowledge of the language and higher cultural level, they must be treated more gently than the Russian Jews. The following data, which paint a picture of how life actually is in the German ghetto, should be of interest: the German Jews in the ghetto number 7000 people. Of these 1800 are capable of working. Of these around 900 people cannot at present be used for work due to diseases linked to malnourishment. The diseases are, in general, the following:

370	dysentery
102	frostbite
135	festering wounds
210	conjunctival inflammation of the eyes
25	pneumonia
63	influenza and rheumatic diseases
30	diseases of the bladder

This is the data as of the 31st of December 1941. Diseases equivalent to those listed above are also present in the ghetto for Russian Jews with the difference that the percentage of those suffering from them is acknowledged by all to be higher.

Cont'd

The German Jews in Minsk are especially grateful for the care shown to them by the Chief Commissar Gauleiter Kube. Kube, while on a visit… to the ghetto in November 1941 he discovered that the relatives of some of the Jews were fighting on the front. Wishing to follow up on this matter, he promised to report it to the führer of the ghetto for the Berlin Jews.

Gauleiter Kube's attention was caught by two Jewish girls who looked Aryan. He ordered a political leader to establish the identity of the girls and have them dismissed from the ghetto. One of the girls then went on to work in the General Commissariat, combining work as a stenographer with hairdressing; she was also exempted from wearing a "star" so as not to offend Germans whose hair she was cutting or arouse their displeasure on seeing a Jewish "star".

An elder of the Jewish ghetto was received by the General Commissar and was given ample opportunity to voice his complaints. Prior to this his deputy had been complaining that one of the older members of the Party was threatening to beat him up and even to put a bullet through his head. Numerous complaints were also filed by the Jewish Council against the Hautsturmführer [sic] of the headquarters of the SS and the Chiefs of Police for beating up Jews whose work was not satisfactory.

Taking into consideration the multiple reports filed by the Jewish Council on the extreme malnourishment suffered by inhabitants of the ghetto the possibility of transferring responsibility for supplies and upkeep to the Wehrmacht was raised. The head of the financial department of the Wehrmacht also announced that based on the food supplies which the Wehrmacht currently holds, the upkeep of 7000 Jews should not pose any difficulties.

On their arrival in Minsk, most of the German Jews supposed that they were being brought here with the aim of colonising eastern territories. But after they had been herded into the ghetto and subjected to a long period of poor treatment, rumours began to spread that their resettlement was a temporary measure and that after the end of the war they would be allowed to return to Germany. This belief, which helped them to overcome the difficulties of daily life, is the one held by most Jews; only an insignificant minority were aware of what their actual fate would be, and these people do not dare to talk about it out loud.

Cont'd

In these circumstances, like in others, the Jews have shown their amazing and characteristic ability to adapt, putting it to use to make their lives a little easier. For example, the Bruners organised a variety show as best they could and gathered a reasonably good crowd.

Judging by the conversations of the Jews themselves it can be concluded that sexual activity is still going on in the ghetto. It is hard to tell whether this is an end in itself or out of concern for producing a robust next generation.

The large concentration of Jews within a small space inside the ghetto has naturally created favourable conditions for the spread of infectious diseases.

With the onset of early spring, it is important to take this into account, as the ghetto is a haven for infectious diseases from which such diseases could cross over not only into the Belorussian population but also to German citizens and soldiers.

The campaign for woollen items carried out in January 1942 inside the German ghetto yielded the following results:

Coats – 329
Jackets – 159
Items made of fur – 128
Sleeve warmers – 300
Fur collars – 2146
Fur hats – 100
Boas (collars) – 440

Even if it made economic sense, the destruction of Jews in large numbers would be impossible at present due to climatic conditions: the ground is frozen stiff which makes digging graves and filling them in unfeasible.

Burckhard [sic]

Obersturmführer of the SS and Criminal Commissar

National Archive of the Republic of Belarus. F. 1216. Op. 1. Document 3. Sheets 253-261. Translated from German.

Protocol: surveying the sites of mass burials in the area of the Jewish cemetery in Minsk

24th July 1944

I, doctor Melnikova Yevgeniya Ivanovna, in the presence of Ioffe, an engineer and land surveyor for the Shafranskiy Minsk District Land Department and local resident, have conducted a survey of the location detailed above and discovered the following information as below.

On the southern and south-western sides of the cemetery 4 mass graves have been found located by the road leading out of the centre of Minsk to the Tuchinka boundary, 2 metres from the road. Three of these run parallel to the road on the south-western side, and the fourth at an angle to them on the southern side.

On measurement, the graves were found to be of the following dimensions:

First grave: 18 metres long by 5 metres wide
Second grave: 14 metres long by 5.5 metres wide
Third grave: 15 metres long by 5.5 metres wide
Fourth grave: 18 metres long by 6 metres wide

On investigation of the immediate surroundings, it has proven impossible to discover any other graves since public infrastructure has been built over the area. That there are indeed other pits has confidently been confirmed by witnesses of the building activities, which unearthed a massive quantity of corpses.

State Archive of the Minsk Region. F. 7021. Op. 87. Document 123. Sheet 85

Section 4

Photos

Anna Machiz (centre) with her brother, Savely and mother, Frida. Minsk, 191

Frida (mother) with her daughter, Anna, Anna's brother, Savely (standing), Anna Kugel, her mother's cousin. Village of Rusakovichi, 1917

Anna Machiz. Minsk, 1926

Anna Machiz. Minsk, 1927

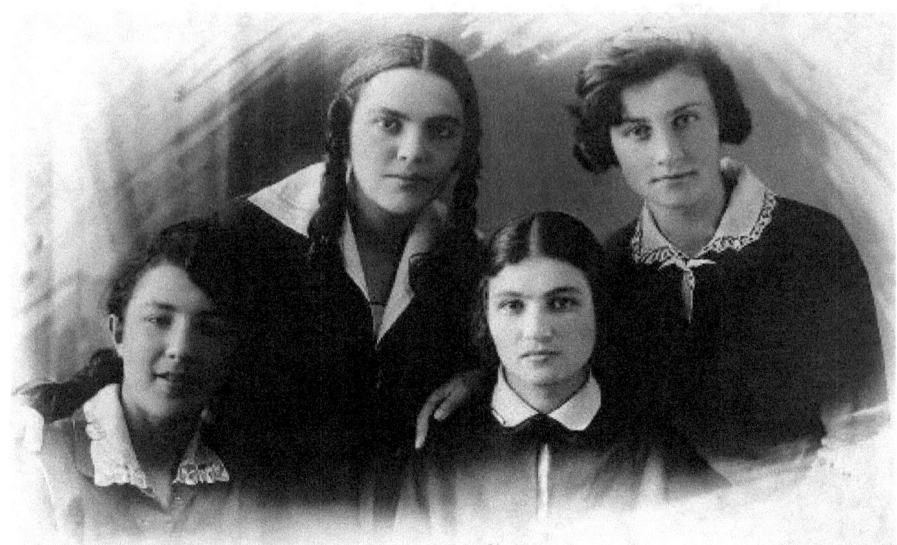

Anna Machiz (centre) with her friends, Musia, Niura and Ida. Minsk, 1928-1930

Anna Machiz. Minsk, 1929

Anna Machiz's brother, Savely. Town of Orekhov, 1941

Anna Machiz. Minsk, 1944

Hersh Smolar

The Minsk Ghetto, 1941-1943

Prisoners of the Minsk Ghetto

Ziama Serebrianskiy

Matvei Pruslin

Khasia Pruslina, 1942

Mikhail Gebelev, Minsk Ghetto Jewish Resistance

Roza Lipskaya

Anna Machiz's temporary ID, 1944

Monument on the site of the last battle fought by the 106th Jewish Partisan detachment. Ivenetskiy district, 1978

Anna Machiz's ID card for External Assignments, 1944

ID card of Anna Machiz, an official of the Prosecutor's Office of the BSSR, 1945

Anna Machiz's permit, 1945

Anna Machiz. Minsk, 1946

Boris Feldman - son of Sara Levina and Detachment Commissar Naum Feldman, 1950

Leonid Tsyrinskiy, Leonid Frid, Sonia Tsyrinskaya. Minsk, 1945

Brother Savely Machiz with his wife Basia, 1948

Anna Machiz's friends and colleagues (first row: Roza Lipskaya) Minsk, 1953

The department for letters at the newspaper Zorka (Anna Machiz is first on the left in the second row), 1947

Anna Machiz and her husband Isaac Levin on holiday, 1954

Anna Machiz's nephew Yevgeny, 1952

Anna Tsyrinskaya and her granddaughter Marina and son Leonid, 1972

Anna Tsyrinskaya with her granddaughter Marina, 1968

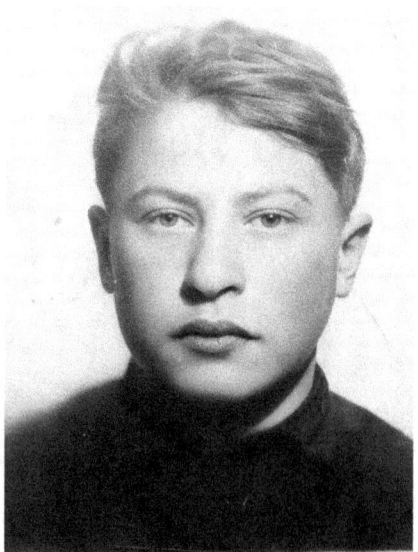

Leonid Tsyrinskiy, 1957

Anna Machiz's niece Sofya Tsyrinskaya, 1958

Sheet one of two from Anna Machiz's memoirs typed on a typewriter in the forest when she was a partisan. Accounts of what she had witnessed in the Minsk Ghetto.

Sheet two of two from Anna Machiz's memoirs typed on a typewriter in the forest when she was a partisan. Accounts of what she had witnessed in the Minsk Ghetto.

- 10 -

Врач детского дома Анна Турецкая, когда ее привезли на кладбище для расстрела, заявила: "Я не боюсь вас. Стреляйте! Наши придут и отомстят за нас!". Расстреляли. В общую могилу скинули. Похитили ее труп из общей могилы и похоронили в отдельной могиле.

По указанию командиров партизанских отрядов, дислоцирующихся в Налибокской пуще, узнавших гетто под разными предлогами выводили в отряды: старики, женщины, дети. Организовался особый отряд в 600 человек. Среди них образовалась боевая группа, которая воевала с врагом: ходили на железную дорогу, на шоссе, уничтожали врагов.

В другие отряды направлялись портные, оружейные мастера, врачи, в том числе была направлена в бригаду им. Дунова на работу в особый отдел автор настоящих записок — Мачиз Анна — б. следователь по важнейшим делам Прокуратуры БССР.

20.XI-1981 г. Первое воспоминание было написано в ноябре 1943 г. в партизанском отряде. *(подпись)* /А. Мачиз/

Continuation of Anna Machiz's memoirs that she wrote in 1981 upon the request of an archivist named Kuprianova.

Confirmation letter by Sarah Levina, a comrade of Anna Machiz written on 21st January 1974 stating that she has known Anna Machiz since 1942 when they fought together against the Nazis. The letter confirms that Leonid Tsyrinskiy is the only nephew of Anna Machiz (son of her sister), and that he was fully under Anna's guardianship.

Testimonies of Tragedy and Resistance in the Minsk Ghetto   133

Anna Levina's ID card, 1964

Partisan ID card of Anna Levina Machiz

By the Monument to the Righteous. Village of Porechye, 2011

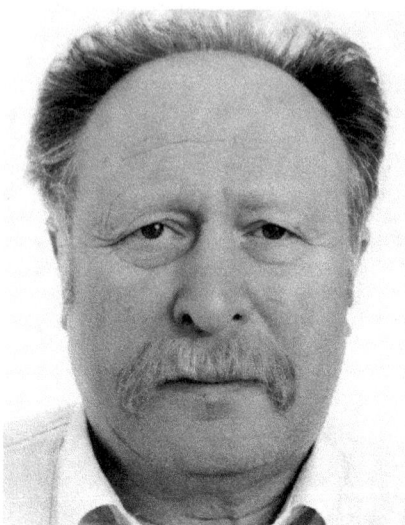

Leonid Tsyrinskiy, 2010

Leonid Tsyrinskiy working on the manuscript, 2011

Leonid Tsyrinskiy with his grandsons Vadim, Mark, and granddaughter Milana, 2010

Anna Machiz. Minsk, 1975

Glossary of terms

Abwehr [German: defence] – The German military intelligence service.

Aktion – See: **Pogrom**.

(The) Black Book [Russian: *Chyornaya Kniga*] – A collection of documents and the testimonies of witnesses of crimes committed by Nazis against the Jews in occupied Poland and the **USSR**. It was compiled by Ilya Ehrenburg and Vasiliy Grossman in the 1940s and not published during their lifetimes.

BSSR – Byelorussian Soviet Socialist Republic. One of the 15 constituent republics of the **USSR**. Following the fall of the Soviet Union in 1991, it gained its current name of the Republic of Belarus.

Candidate of Sciences [Russian: *Kandidat nauk*] – The equivalent of a PhD, awarded in the USSR and to this day in many post-Soviet states including Belarus.

Council of People's Commissars [Russian: Sovet narodnykh kommissarov] – A government institution formed shortly after the October revolution of 1917 which evolved to become the greatest executive authority in the government of the USSR.

Desyatka – A group of ten people. These groups were organised on the basis of their specific assignment: to source weaponry, to distribute food, to carry out medical duties etc. The tenth member was the head of the group.

Doctor of Sciences [Russian: *Doktor nauk*] – A post-doctoral degree awarded in the USSR and to this day in many post-Soviet states including Belarus. It is the next academic level above the Candidate of Sciences (see above).

Dushegubka [Russian: soul-destroyer] – The Russian name given to the mobile gas chambers on wheels which the Nazis would use to conduct pogroms. People would be forcibly loaded into an airtight compartment inside these vehicles, then exhaust gas was pumped in until everyone suffocated.

Einsatzgruppen [German: task forces] – Nazi death squads which played a central role in implementing the so-called 'final solution to the Jewish Question'. After the war, many of their leaders were prosecuted for crimes against humanity or war crimes and sentenced to death or life imprisonment.

Einsatzkommando – A subgroup of the Einsatzgruppen (see above) which carried out the extermination of Jews, Polish intellectuals, Romani, and communists in territories which had already been captured by the Nazis, such as Belarus.

Gebelev, Mikhail (1905- 1942) – An anti-Nazi resistance leader in the Minsk Ghetto. He liaised between the communist resistance movement outside of the ghetto and the ghetto fighters led by Hersh Smolar.

Great Patriotic War [Russian: *Velikaya Otechestvennaya Voyna*] – The term most commonly used by Russians to talk about the Second World War.

(The) Great Victory [Russian: *Velikaya Pobeda*] – The USSR's victory over Nazi Germany in 1945. In Belarus, Russian and other ex-Soviet countries this day is celebrated with a public holiday every year on the 9th of May.

Hamburg Jews – After the two pogroms of 7 and 20 November 1941, trainloads of Jews from Central Europe, many from Hamburg, arrived in Minsk. Many were shot upon arrival and the rest, numbering several thousands, were brought into the Minsk Ghetto, where a special area (a separate 'ghetto within a ghetto') had been 'cleared' and then fenced with barbed wire in order to house them. Contact between these people and the general ghetto population was forbidden.

Judenrat [German: Jewish Council] – A council of Jews appointed by the Germans to be responsible for the internal administration of the ghetto.

KGB (SSSR) [Russian: *Komitet gosudarstvennoy bezopasnosti SSSR*, The Committee for State Security of the USSR] – A secret police force and the main security agency for the Soviet Union from 1954 until its dissolution. It was a successor of the NKVD (see below). Unlike Russia, present-day Belarus still uses the name of KGB for its intelligence agency.

Komsomol(ets) – See: **VLKSM**.

Krasnoye – A village located approximately 16 km south-east of Molodechno (about 57 km from Minsk). A Jewish Ghetto existed there from 1941-1944; it occupied a small area in the centre of the village. In 1942, Jews from Bukovina and Bessarabia were brought there. In March 1944 survivors of this ghetto were liberated.

Kube, Wilhelm (1887-1943) – Generalkommissar for Byelorussia in the occupying government of the Soviet Union. His headquarters were in Minsk, He was assassinated in his Minsk apartment on September 22, 1943.

Labour Market [Russian: *birzha truda*] – A department of the *Judenrat* responsible for supplying labour to meet the demands of the German occupiers.

Malina [Russian: 'raspberry (bush)'] – The code word for 'hiding place'. It has been suggested that the word was chosen to describe a place of concealment in the ghetto because, in this region, raspberry bushes were traditionally well covered during the sub-zero temperatures of winter in order to protect them from frost. For the people of the ghetto, as for the plants, concealment was a matter of survival.

NKVD – Refers to the People's Commissariat of Internal Affairs – The Communist Secret Police.

October Revolution – Also called the Bolshevik Revolution, (Oct. 24–25 [Nov. 6–7, New Style], 1917), was the second and last major phase of the Russian Revolution of 1917, in which Vladimir Lenin's Bolshevik Party seized power in Russia, inaugurating the Soviet regime.

Partisan detachment – The main organisational form of the Soviet partisan units. The bigger detachment in certain conditions could be expanded into a partisan brigade, or into a partisan regiment. Jewish partisans were fighters in irregular military groups participating in the Jewish resistance movement against Nazi Germany and its collaborators during World War II.

Patriotic War – See: **Great Patriotic War**.

Pogrom (in German *Aktion*) – The word originates from the Russian. A pogrom is an organized massacre. In the Minsk ghetto, while random killings were taking place constantly, there were a series of pogroms as follows:

7 Nov 1941 – The First pogrom
20 Nov 1941 – The second pogrom

2-3 March 1942 – The third pogrom held at the time of Purim (a celebration of Jewish deliverance as told in the Book of Esther). This pogrom included the massacre at Yama (see Yama below).
April - May 1942 – A series of small, organized actions
28-31 July 1942 – The fourth pogrom – this was the largest pogrom. It lasted for four days. All of the non-working population of the ghetto was destroyed. Estimates of the numbers killed range from 18,000 to 30,000 with around 12,000 remaining live in the ghetto.
21 Oct 1943 – The fifth pogrom and final liquidation of the ghetto. There are no precise figures for those remaining alive, but estimates are less than 100.

Polizei – The German police.

Porechye – A village in the Minsk region. In late 1943 it became a destination for Jewish children escaping the Minsk ghetto with assistance from the partisans. The lives of many of the children were saved by village families and individuals who accommodated and cared for them at that time. A monument in honour of those courageous people was unveiled there in 2000.

Russian District – This was the area of Minsk, located outside the barbed wire perimeter of the Minsk Ghetto.

SD Full title: *Sicherheitsdienst des Reichsführers.* – An organization which was, in effect, the intelligence agency of the SS, the Nazi Secret Police.

Smolar, Hersh (Smolyar, Girsh/Grisha) (1905-1993) – A Polish and Soviet Yiddish writer and editor. He was a leading member of underground resistance in the Minsk ghetto and became commissar of a partisan group operating in Byelorussian forests. His wartime memoirs, *Fun Minsker geto* [Yiddish: From the Minsk Ghetto], were published in 1946.

Tuchinka – An execution area outside of Minsk. On 7 November 1941 (the date of the first pogrom in the Minsk Ghetto) thousands of Jews, probably numbering between 12,000 and 17,000 in total, were marched from the ghetto to Tuchinka and shot. On 20 November, a second pogrom took place when a further 5000 to 10000 Jews from the ghetto were also massacred at Tuchinka.

Trostenets – A World War II Nazi German death camp and burial site located near the village of Maly Trostenets on the outskirts of Minsk. It operated between July 1942 and October 1943, by which time virtually all Jews remaining in Minsk had been murdered. While Jews were brought to Trostenets from across Austria, Germany and the Czech Republic, the primary purpose of the camp was the killing by firing squad and mobile gas chambers of Jewish prisoners of the Minsk Ghetto and the surrounding area. A memorial site opened at Maly Trostenets in 2015.

Underground – In October 1941, groups of Jewish communists inside the Minsk Ghetto formed an underground organization with the aim of transferring people from the ghetto to partisan groups in the forests. [See above, **Hirsh Smolar**].

USSR – Union of Soviet Socialist Republics [Russian: Soyuz Sovetskikh Sotsialisticheskikh Respublik or Sovetsky Soyuz]. Former northern Eurasian empire (1917/22–1991) stretching from the Baltic and Black seas to the Pacific Ocean and, in its final years, consisting of 15 Soviet Socialist Republics (SSR's).

VLKSM – A Russian acronym for *Vsesoyuzny Leninskiy Kommunisticheskiy Soyuz Molodyozhi*: The All-Union Leninist Young Communist League (1981-1991), often abbreviated to *Komsomol*. A member was known as a *komsomolets*; they were aged 14-28 and membership was nominally voluntary. The *Komsomol* played an important part in teaching the values of the Communist Party and the Soviet Union to youngsters. Active members received privileges and preferences in promotion.

Western Belarus – Part of the Second Polish Republic during the inter-war years. After World War II the area was ceded to the Soviet Union by the Allied Powers.

Work Detail – Most able-bodied adult Jews from the Minsk Ghetto were assigned to groups with whom they would work regularly outside of the Ghetto, in the Russian District. In these stories, this kind of group is generally referred to as a 'Work Detail'. The groups would be marched out of the Ghetto each morning under armed guard and transported to various workplaces in or around Minsk. Some workers were employed to carry out menial tasks such as the clearing of rubble on building sites. There were also a number of 'specialist' groups, from needlewomen to factory workers and skilled technicians. The workers sometimes received limited food rations which some took home at the end of the day to share with their starving families inside the ghetto.

Yama – The word in Byelorussian means 'the pit' and refers to an area inside the Minsk Ghetto which had originally been a quarry bordering on Ratomskaya Street. It has now given its name to a monument which marks the location of the largest punitive action to have been conducted in the Ghetto: In early 1942 the Jewish council of the Ghetto was ordered by the German authorities to gather together 5000 Jews for deportation. When news of the order spread, many of the ghetto inhabitants went into hiding. On 2 March it became obvious that the quota of 5000 people had not been fulfilled. German security forces consisting of Byelorussians, Lithuanians, and Ukrainians then entered the ghetto and began randomly taking people. Many were shot trying to hide or escape. More than 5000 people were taken to the large pit on Ratomskaya Street and shot.

The memorial, which now marks this location consists of an obelisk which was created in 1947, and a bronze sculpture created in in 2000, entitled 'The Last Way'. It represents a group of people, walking down steps to their doom in the pit. The sculpture was created by Belarusian artist and Chairman of the Jewish communities of Belarus, Leonid Levin (1936-2014) together with Israeli sculptor Elsa Pollak. On the obelisk, in Russian and Yiddish, appear the words "The bright memory of five times the light of thousands of Jews who perished at the hands of sworn enemies of humanity - German-fascist monsters."

Yellow Patch – Refers to the circular pieces of yellow fabric, which Jews in the Minsk Ghetto were ordered to wear. The order applied to everyone over the age of ten. The patches were to be 10cm in diameter and attached to the outer garments, on both the left side of the chest, and on the back. Many of the Minsk Jews referred to the patches in Yiddish, as *lata* or *laty*. (In Yiddish transliteration as standardised by YIVO, the Institute for Jewish Research, the word is spelled '*late*', but we have employed '*lata*' or '*laty*' here to avoid confusion with pronunciation).

In some photographs, Jews in the Minsk Ghetto can also be seen wearing the yellow star, or armbands displaying the Star of David. These would probably have been worn by Jews who had been transported to Minsk from other areas in Europe (see **Hamburg Jews**).

Zorin's Brigade – A Byelorussian partisan unit, led by Simcha (Sholem) Zorin. In June 1941 Zorin had escaped from the Minsk Ghetto and fled to the forests to join the partisans operating in the Staroye Selo region, about 19 miles southwest of Minsk. Toward the end of 1942, it was becoming apparent that the Red Army would ultimately prevail, but that the

Germans would destroy the Minsk Ghetto before retreating. In early 1943, in the Staroselskiy Forest close to Minsk, Zorin obtained permission from partisan leaders to form a new unit which would not only offer protection to the growing number of refugees coming out of the Minsk Ghetto, but also actively bring out more people. The unit was called the 106th. It consisted of an armed unit of partisan fighters, and also welcomed children, the elderly and the infirm. It ultimately totalled around 800 Jews. After the liquidation of the Minsk Ghetto, the brigade moved to the Naliboki Forest where it survived to the end of the war. In 1956, a monument was erected in the Naliboki Forest to the memory of the fighters of the 106th Battalion.

Zorka [Russian: ray of dawn/dusk light] – A Belarusian children's newspaper founded in Minsk in 1944.

Gallery of archive images

Persecution of Jews by the Nazi occupation forces in the BSSR. In the photo: Minsk Jews during snow removal at the railway station. February 1942.
Photo attribution: Bundesarchiv, Bild 183-B07892 / Donath, Herbert / CC-BY-SA 3.0

Occupied territories by Nazi troops. Forced labour of the Jewish population on the icy platform of the Minsk wagon depot. February 1942.
Photo Attribution: Bundesarchiv, Bild 183-N1213-348 / Donath, Herbert / CC-BY-SA 3.0

Nazi-occupied territories. Forced labour of the Jewish population on the railway. Minsk, BSSR. February 1942.
Photo Attribution: Bundesarchiv, Bild 183-N1213-361 / Donath, Herbert / CC-BY-SA 3.0

Erich von dem Bach Zelewski - German SS-Obergruppenführer, General of the Waffen-SS and General of the Police instrumental in the Holocaust and later as "Head of the Gang Combat Associations" in the mass murder campaigns involved in the Soviet Union. He was responsible for the Einsatzgruppe B unit that massacred Jews in Belorussia.
Photo attribution: Bundesarchiv, Bild 101III-Weiss-046-14 / Weiss / CC-BY-SA 3.0

From Communiqué No. 31 of the Security Police and the SD on the creation of the Jewish Council (Judenrat)

> *23rd July 1941*
>
> ...as the German soldier cannot always unfailingly distinguish Jewish people from non-Jewish local population, in some cases misunderstandings have occurred. A regulation has therefore been issued requiring that with immediate effect, Jewish men and women aged 10 and older wear yellow sewn-on patches on their breasts and backs at all times.

National Archive of the Republic of Belarus. Fond 4683 OP3 D943 L88-89
Translated from German.

Belarusian Jews in the Minsk Ghetto were ordered to wear a yellow patch by the German Security Police and the Sicherheitsdienst (SD, Security Service of the Reichsführer-SS). The order applied to everyone over the age of ten (see the order below). The patches were to be 10cm in diameter and attached to the outer garments, on both the left side of the chest, and on the back. The prisoners referred to the patches in Yiddish as "late", pronounced: 'lata' or 'laty' (see glossary).

Photo attribution: Bundesarchiv N 1576 Bild-006, Minsk, Juden-remini-enhanced, Herrmann, Ernst, CC BY-SA 3.0 via Wikimedia Commons

Murdered Soviets - photograph believed to have been taken in Minsk.
Photo attribution: Bundesarchiv, Bild 146-1970-043-52 / CC-BY-SA 3.0

German infantry and motorized troops marching through a village near Minsk, August 1941
Photo attribution: Bundesarchiv, Bild 101I-138-1068-06 / Dreyer / CC-BY-SA 3.0

Testimonies of Tragedy and Resistance in the Minsk Ghetto 147

Persecution of Jews by the Nazi occupation forces in the BSSR. Jewish citizens of Minsk clearing snow at the railway station, February 1942.
Photo attribution: Bundesarchiv, Bild 183-B07894 / Donath, Herbert / CC-BY-SA 3.0

Index of names

A

Adams, 11, 13, 22
Alpert, iv
Arad, 13, 23
Armyaninov, 42
Arotsker, 93

B

Baker, ii, 11, 13, 11
Balakirev, 8
Balakirov, 30
Baranovsky, 46
Baratz, 80, 81
Basin, 30
Baum, 11, 90
Belostokskiy, 82
Benya, 94, 103
Berson, 93
Bindler, 92
Blacher, 82
Blumenstock, 72
Blumin, 82, 83
Botvinnik, 35
Bozhenko, 40
Bronstein, 11, 19, 23
Bruk, 31
Brunner, ii, 11, 13, 4, 19
Bruskin, 35
Bruskind, 60
Brustin, 92, 95
Budyonny, 70, 93, 94, 102
Bunge, 74, 77, 78, 79, 94
Burckhard, 114
Burckhardt, 113
Burshtyn, 35
Bystrov, 57, 89

C

Chaimovich, 30
Chauskaya-Ilyashova, 31
Chepik, 95
Cherepanov, 9
Cherno, 53
Chernoglazova, 30
Chkalov, 94
Cohen, 18, 23
Croz, 31

D

Davydova, 31
Demby, 19, 23
Donath, 142, 143, 146
Dreyer, 145
Dudkovskiy, 40, 41, 42, 45
Dukorskiy, 81, 82
Dzerzhinskiy, 94
Dzyadzyudya, 103, 104

E

Ehrenburg, 27, 34, 135
Eisenburg, 51
Epstein, 14, 19, 23, 30, 49, 63, 64, 70, 75, 76, 77, 78, 79, 80, 83, 84, 90, 94

F

Feigelman, 102
Feinstein, iv
Feldman, 27, 35, 56, 61, 62, 65, 66, 69, 70, 90, 93, 95, 102, 124
Fichtel, 68, 73
Finski, 30
Fiterson, 27, 103
Flanagan, 8
Frid, 26, 124
Frunze, 94

G

Galburt, 30
Galperina, 31
Ganzenko, 70, 94
Gattenbach, 71, 72, 73, 75
Gavi, 31
Gaysarov, 40
Gazenko, 93
Gebelev, 33, 35, 37, 57, 60, 65, 66, 70, 88, 90, 92, 93, 95, 121, 136

Gerasimova, 31
Gimpel, 94, 103
Ginter, 77
Ginzburg, 63, 70, 77, 94
Gleizer, 34
Goldin, 58
Goldman, 94
Gordon, 57
Gorelik, 92
Gorodetskiy, 55, 58
Gorshenin, 43, 44
Göttenbach, 67, 68
Graivors, 52
Grechanik, 34
Grichannik, 95
Groll, iii
Grossman, 27, 34, 135
Grunfest, 68
Gurevich, 35
Gurvich, 35, 71, 95
Gusinov, 35
Guy, 27, 37, 46, 98

H

Hecker, 30
Herrmann, 144
Hertzig, 35
Hertzik, 93
Hitler, 1, 51, 53, 56, 57, 59, 62, 72, 78, 83, 95, 99

I

Ilinskiy, 79
Ioffe, 13, 20, 21, 30, 34, 66, 72, 90
Ivanov, 82, 83
Ivanovna, 115

J

Junge-Wentrup,, 8

K

Kagal, 70
Kagan, 18, 23, 35, 63, 77, 92, 94
Kaganovitch, 17, 23
Kantorovich, 71

Kantsevaya, 78
Kapilovich, 85, 102
Kaplan, 54, 93
Kaplinsky, 31
Kaydalov, 40
Kazhdan, 35
Khaimovich, 35, 56, 102
Khankovich, 57
Kiriyeshto, 57
Kirkoyeshto, 33, 35
Klara, 31, 92
Klebanova, 94, 103
Kleonskiys, 52
Klionskiy, 94, 103
Kovalyov, 82
Kozak, 8, 13, 8, 20, 28, 30, 31
Krapina, 31
Krasnoperko, 31
Kravchinskiy, 102
Kroshner, 71
Kube, 113, 137
Kudryakov, 91
Kugel, 26, 118
Kulik, 35, 93
Kupreeva, 30, 38
Kutuzov, 94
Kuzir, 61
Kuzmin, 82

L

Langbard, 52
Lapidus, 30, 69
Larno, 72
Lazo, 94, 102
Leli, 31
Lenin, 137
Lev, 35, 79
Levin, 8, 27, 30, 31, 35, 64, 126, 140
Levina, 13, 27, 31, 34, 35, 37, 38, 46, 88, 124, 131, 132
Levine, 3
Libo, 92
Lipskaya, 27, 35, 121, 125
Liss, 62, 65, 92, 95
Livshits, 69
Livshyts, 11, 12, 2
Loewenstein, 31
Logvinov, 8

Losik, 35, 95

M

Machiz, i, ii, 7, 8, 12, 13, 3, 5, 6, 7, 8, 10, 11, 15, 16, 18, 19, 20, 21, 24, 26, 28, 29, 33, 34, 35, 36, 37, 38, 41, 42, 43, 44, 45, 46, 47, 50, 87, 88, 96, 97, 98, 99, 103, 117, 118, 119, 120, 122, 123, 124, 125, 126, 127, 128, 129, 130, 131, 132, 134
Maizelis, 93
Maizels, 61, 71, 90, 95
Maizles, 35
Margolin, 61
Margolina, 31, 54
Markevich, 93
Markin, 70
Markman, 63, 77, 94
Mekhovskiy, 82
Melnitskiy, 11, 13, 7
Melomed, 31
Mendel, 73, 92
Menschel, 68
Menzel, 81
Michelson, 73, 74, 75, 76, 78, 79, 80, 94, 100, 101
Miller, 73, 75, 80
Mindel, 35
Minkin, 93
Mirkin, 35, 92
Monisov, 37, 98, 99
Mushkin, 52, 58, 62, 89, 90

N

Naliboki Forest, 3, 20, 22, 34, 85, 96, 141
Nalibokskiy, 35
Neu, 75, 76, 101
Nikitin, 69, 70
Nyman, 11

O

Ohnenheim, 61
Okun, 35, 57, 61, 66, 90, 91, 103
Ost, 15

P

Paleyev, 68
Parkhomenko, 85
Pechmann, 78
Pevsner, 95
Podoprigora, 93
Pollak, 30, 140
Prischepkin, 93
Pruslin, 33, 35, 89, 92, 121
Pruslina, 31, 33, 35, 121
Pryklad, 51
Prytykin, 51

R

Rapoport, 31
Rapoports, 52
Reizman, 5, 19, 31
Reutskiy, 81
Ribbe, 73, 74, 75, 76, 77, 78, 79, 80, 81, 84, 85, 94, 100, 101
Richter, 63, 64, 67, 68, 73, 81
Rodova, 61, 90, 93
Rodovaya, 33, 35
Rodzinskiy, 30
Rolbin, 35, 61, 90, 93
Rosenberg, 31
Rosenblat, 63, 70, 74, 90, 94
Rosin, iv, 11
Rubenchik, 30, 31, 37, 49, 61, 90
Rubin, 35
Ruditskiy, 90
Rudovich, 93

S

Sadovskaya, 38
Samuil, 35, 77
Sarin, 64
Savchik, 79
Savich, 81
Savvina, 79
Schedletskiy, 93
Scherner, 74, 77, 78, 79, 84, 94
Schmidt, 63, 64
Schnittman, 56, 57
Schultz, 78, 95
Schusser, 90

Selemenev, 31
Semyonovna, 13, 24, 26, 27, 35, 37, 38, 39, 40, 41, 43, 44, 45, 46, 88, 98
Serebrianskiy, 121
Serebryanskiy, 37, 58, 89, 98
Shafran, 93
Shafranskiy, 115
Shaipak, 11
Shapiro, 34, 95
Shlyakhtovich, 35
Shmotkin, 79
Shmotkina, 79
Silberstein, 82, 95
Sirotkina, 71
Siterman, 55
Skachkov, 70
Skakun, 4, 30
Skoblo, 62
Slavek', 60
Smilovistsky, 17, 23
Smolar, 27, 29, 33, 34, 35, 37, 56, 60, 65, 66, 90, 120, 136, 138, 139
Smolyar, 138
Snyder, 1
Speakman, 11
Speer, 99
Stakhanov, 62
Stalin, 21, 38, 45, 52, 70, 93, 94
Stolyarevich, 60, 66, 90, 95, 102
Stolyarevich', 66
Sukenik, 95
Sulthan, 11
Svinovskaya, 99

T

Taubkina, 54
Traister, 30
Trapp, ii, 11, 13, 3, 9
Treister, 30
Trugel, 71
Tsyrinskaya, 24, 26, 124, 127

Tsyrinskiy, i, ii, 8, 10, 11, 13, 2, 3, 20, 21, 26, 29, 33, 34, 35, 38, 45, 46, 102, 103, 104, 124, 127, 131, 133
Tukala, 32
Tukalo, 32
Tulskiy, 95
Tumin, 69
Tunik, 93
Turetskaya, 83, 96

V

Vasilevich, 40, 42
Vetrov, 44
Villigst, 31
Vinnitsa, 32
Vintkyevich, 45
Von Bechtolsheim, 109
Voroshilovskiy, 60, 89
Vovka, 93

W

Wade-Beorn, 13, 17, 23
Walke, 14, 15, 16, 18, 23
Weinhaus, 35, 56, 57, 60, 88, 89
Weiss, 143

Y

Yankovich, 96

Z

Zabel, 8
Zavolner, 31
Zelewski, 143
Zheleznyak, 92
Zhenka, 35
Zhitelzey, 93
Zhits, 49
Zhukov, 21, 36, 38, 41, 42, 45, 96
Zorin, 85, 140
Zuckerman, 11
Zyama, 37, 61, 90, 91, 98, 99

www.ingramcontent.com/pod-product-compliance
Lightning Source LLC
Chambersburg PA
CBHW051748230426
43670CB00012B/2204